MILITARY POWER

USMC

RUSS BRYANT AND W. DAVID PERKS

ZENITH PRESS

Dedication

I would like to dedicate my work on this book to my dad, Jerry Perks, who has the spirit of a warrior. In many ways, his battles began on September 11, 2001, and he continues to fight them all with courage.

—Dave Perks

ISBN-13: 978-0-7603-2532-2
ISBN-10: 0-7603-2532-4

Editors: Lindsay Hitch and Steve Gansen
Designer: Brenda C. Canales

Printed in China

About the authors:
Russ Bryant is a veteran of 1st Ranger Battalion from 1985 to 1989. Following his service, Bryant attended Savannah College of Art and Design and received a Bachelors of Fine Art Degree in Photography. As a photographer and ranger veteran, his passions quite naturally led him to photograph rangers in the tactical environment. He has photographed the 75th Ranger Regiment extensively over the last several years, including the 1st Ranger Battalion at Hunter Army Air Field, the 3rd Ranger Battalion at Fort Benning, and the 2nd Ranger Battalion at Fort Lewis, Washington.

W. David Perks has written for the official Marine Corps web site, Marines.com, and for numerous USMC promotional materials. He has a Master's Degree in Mass Communications from Virginia Commonwealth University. Perks lives in McDonough, Georgia, with his wife, Sara, and his son, Jayme.

On the cover: Recruits charge with fixed bayonets in a photo that is reminiscent of a memorable page in Marine Corps history, when men from B Company, 1/26 charged a North Vietnamese position outside the firebase of Khe Sanh on March 30, 1968. These Marines attacked the position to recover the bodies of fallen brothers from an ambush by the enemy the night before. They recovered the bodies and killed many North Vietnamese soldiers in the process.

On the frontispiece: Captain William G. Rayne, Sergeant Jorge H. Herrera, Lance Corporal Joshua C. Landis, and Lance Corporal Curt L. Smith all received their Purple Heart medals in a ceremony. The Marines were involved in a rocket-propelled grenade attack on their building in the middle of the night.

On the title pages: Marines sweep through rubble and collapsed homes looking for insurgents and weapons caches. The rubble creates excellent firing positions for enemy snipers.

On the back cover: (top) Lance Corporal Michael Oliver Ray (also known as "Thor"), a rifleman in Company B, 1st Battalion, 8th Marine Regiment, Regimental Combat Team 7, kicks down a door while searching the city of Fallujah, Iraq, for insurgents and weapons during Operation Al Fajr.

(bottom) In perfect step, these recruits are a few hours away from becoming U.S. Marines. Many of these young recruits will end up fighting in Iraq and other areas of the Middle East.

Photography Credits:
All Chapter 1 photos by Russ Bryant. Shot digitally with Canon Mark II cameras and Canon lenses.
Thanks to all the Marine combat photographers for the use of their images to help tell the story in Iraq. You are to be commended on a job well done under the most extreme conditions. Semper Fidelis.
Sergeant Stephen D' Alessio, USMC
Corporal Adam C. Schell, USMC
Lance Corporal Sarah A. Beavers, USMC
Sergeant Jose E. Guillen, USMC
Corporal Matthew J. Apprendi, USMC
Corporal Paula M. Fitzgerald, USMC
Corporal Shawn C. Rhodes, USMC
Lance Corporal Samual Bard Valliere, USMC
Corporal Chance W. Haworth, USMC
Corporal Richard Stephens, USMC

Corporal Macario P. Mora Jr., USMC
Lance Corporal Louis Fuentes, USMC
Corporal Paul Leicht, USMC
Corporal Randy L. Bernard, USMC
Corporal Tom Sloan, USMC
Lance Corporal Athanasios L. Genos, USMC
Corporal Neil A. Sevelius, USMC
Corporal Ken Melton, USMC
Corporal Ruben D. Maestre, USMC
Corporal Shane Suzuki, USMC
Corporal Christopher G. Graham, USMC
Staff Sergeant Bryan P. Reed, USMC
Gunnery Sergeant Erik S. Hansen, USMC
Lucian Read, World Picture News
Corporal Anthony R. Blanco, USMC

Contents

FLO

Acknowledgments

I would like to thank the United States Marine Corps. It was an honor to witness such professionalism and dedication to the mission.

Thank you to all the men and women in uniform serving our great country, especially the service personnel in Iraq and Afghanistan.

Thank you to Lieutenant Scott A. Miller, deputy public affairs officer at Parris Island, South Carolina, for the access and making things happen. I extend gratitude to Lieutenant Colonel Darhonda Rodela from Parris Island for all her insight and transportation, and her admonition to always "keep your feet and knees together." I greatly appreciate Lieutenant Colonel Brian Kester, Parris Island, for gathering a highly motivated group of young Marines for the "photo op." Thank you to Lieutenant Colonels Edwin A. Sastano, James M. Shipman, Martin Thomas, and Justin J. Shemanski, all from Parris Island.

I extend my heartfelt appreciation to my wonderful and supportive wife, Susan. Without her, this project would have not happened. I appreciate that my children, Morgan and Travis, understand why I'm always gone shooting photos.

My editor, Steve Gansen, whom I consider a good friend, listens to all of my crazy book proposals, and I could not complete any project without his enthusiasm and continued support. Thanks to MBI Publishing Company for letting us tell a great story and making such high-quality books.

I would like to thank Dave Perks for taking on such a demanding project despite his schedule and crazy deadlines. Dave, you have written an outstanding book, and I am honored to have you on board.

—*Russ Bryant*

I would like to thank the Marine Corps for the work it does and for being so easy to work with. Having had the opportunity to speak with so many Marines, I have an even greater appreciation for the sacrifices you make.

Thank you to Major Donald B. Richwine for getting me in touch with the Marines, who provided many of the stories in this book. I greatly appreciate the time that Majors Pete McAleer and Ryan Paterson set aside to speak with me to provide a few of those stories. And thank you to the others who said their only desire was to tell the story of their Marines, not to have their names published. I hope I made you all proud.

My gratitude goes out to First Sergeant Jamie Karnes and Sergeant Ernest Claiborne for reliving what must have been some painful memories of their time with Mortuary Affairs. Their pride in the work they did was more than evident. I would also like to thank Kip Jarrard, former Marine, for getting me in touch with them.

My deepest and loving appreciation is extended to my incredible wife, Sara, and son, Jayme. Neither one even batted an eye every time I said I had to go work on the book. Their support is what keeps me going.

Steve Gansen and everyone else at MBI Publishing Company, thank you for taking Russ' word that I could write this book. Russ Bryant, thank you for taking my word that I could write this book. I owe you both a deep debt of gratitude for giving me the chance to write my first book.

—*Dave Perks*

Introduction

"Some people spend an entire lifetime wondering if they've made difference. The Marines don't have that problem."

—Ronald Reagan, President of the United States of America

Like most advertising people, I thought I knew all there was to know about the agency's clients I wrote for. So when I was approached about writing a book for one of them, I thought, "No problem." In this instance, the agency was J. Walter Thompson and the client was the United States Marine Corps. The agency had handled the business for decades by the time I even showed up for my first day of work. I then filled in some of the blanks on their marketing efforts for a grand total of eighteen months. Some expert.

Still, I'm glad my over-confidence told me to write USMC. It's taught me many lessons about the Marine Corps and about myself. What I knew about the Marine Corps turned out to be barely enough to complete the first chapter. After that, it was dig, dig, dig.

I have two hopes for USMC. The first is that any Devil Dog who picks it up and thumbs through it sees it as a tribute to his or her work. That's certainly been my intention from the beginning. The second is that anyone else who is inclined to spend time with it learns even a fraction of what I did about what makes the Marine Corps such a unique branch of the U.S. military.

This book does not spend much time on the training process each and every Marine endures. There have been volumes written about that. And while that training is at the heart of every Marine, this text instead explores strategies used by the Marines to turn that training into victory. In the course of researching USMC, my respect for the Corps grew exponentially with every article I read, every Marine I interviewed, and every story I heard.

These men and women exemplify bravery, honor, and commitment in everything they do. It has been my pleasure to bring to light some of the ways in which they do it through both tactical explanations and anecdotal stories. To me, it seemed like the only way to write this book. After all, Marines are famous for their technical expertise and their ability to weave a tale.

—W. David Perks
McDonough, Georgia
November 2005

Chapter 1

THE UNITED STATES MARINE CORPS

AN OVERVIEW

Say what you want to about the United States Marine Corps. But if there's a Marine nearby, you'd better be ready to defend yourself. Nowhere else in the world will you find a military organization that is more widely respected than the U.S. Marines. But this group of men and women, recognized by many as the world's most elite fighting force, is almost as misunderstood as it is revered. Willingly putting yourself in a position to accept untold risk is not an everyday occurrence for most of us. But if you're a member of the Marine Corps, America's force in readiness, it's your job.

Without a doubt, it takes a special person with a unique mindset to answer the call of the Marines. And make no mistake, it is a calling. Marine recruits are among the nation's finest young adults. The Marine Corps was once considered the last chance for those with no other hope for a future, but most current "boots" (Marine slang for new Marines or recruits) had a choice between attending college and sticking out recruit training.

Legendary Marines

Those who came before today's Marines left a legacy that would take generations to replicate. It was men like Chesty Puller, Dan Daly, and Presley O'Bannon who built the legacy that current Marines proudly strive to uphold.

The transformation from civilian to Marine is a short thirteen-week process, but the values that are instilled will last a lifetime. Haircuts mark the start of that transition and establish the recruits with a common denominator. It also helps with personal hygiene.

Opposite: Nuts to butts. The senior drill instructor communicates in a subtle way as fresh recruits line up for the cheapest and quickest haircut they will ever have.

Parris Island trains all females that enter the Marines. The average daily population on Parris Island is 616 females compared to 3,922 males. Female recruits participate in physical training with jumping jacks, hello dollies, pushups, and good morning darlings.

Lieutenant Presley N. O'Bannon

On April 27, 1805, Marine Lieutenant Presley N. O'Bannon led a force of Marines and mercenaries across six hundred miles of the Libyan Desert to attack the fortress at Derne, Tripoli, while naval forces provided bombardment. The attack was in response to the capture and subsequent imprisonment of the 180-man crew of the USS *Philadelphia* by Barbary Coast pirates during the first Tripolitan War. O'Bannon's success led to the first victory of American land forces on foreign soil, and it marked the first time an American flag flew over a captured fortification in the Old World. In appreciation for O'Bannon's services, Hamet Bey, the rightful ruler of Tripoli, presented O'Bannon with his own sword, a curved blade with ivory hilt topped by a golden eagle's head—the Mameluke sword. This sword served as the pattern for those still carried by Marine officers.

Lieutenant General Lewis B. "Chesty" Puller

So nicknamed for his barrel chest, Lieutenant General Puller is one of only two men to have been awarded five Navy Crosses, the second-highest medal awarded by the U.S. Navy and the Marine Corps. Puller also earned the Distinguished Service Cross, the Silver Star, two Legions of Merit, a Bronze Star, Air Medal, and Purple Heart, not to mention numerous awards from governments outside the United States. Collectively, his fifty-two awards and commendations still find Puller at the top of the heap as the most decorated Marine ever. Famous for quotes such as "We're surrounded . . . That simplifies our problem," he is honored by many Marines who still end their day by saying, "Good night, Chesty, wherever you are."

Gunnery Sergeant Dan Daly

Gunnery Sergeant Daly is one of two Marines to have received two Medals of Honor for two separate acts of heroism. In June 1918, right before ordering a history-making attack at Belleau Wood, Daly delivered one of the most famous battle cries. Outnumbered, outgunned, and under siege, he urged his troops to battle by shouting, "Come on, you sons of bitches. Do you want to live forever?" It was during that fight that Daly earned the Navy Cross. His other commendations include the Distinguished Service Cross, the French Medaille Militaire, the Croix du Guerre with Palm, and the Fourragere. Daly turned down several officer

Female recruits in their third week of training walk to cool down from physical training. This particular morning, the women climbed ropes and negotiated an obstacle course.

Below: Every training session starts with blocks of instruction by the drill instructors. Recruits are listening to a class on hand-to-hand combat, which they will execute and practice on one another.

On the Recruit Physical Fitness Test, male recruits must run three miles in under twenty-eight minutes, and females must make the same run in under thirty-one minutes. The average score for male recruits is 229 points, and for females it is 272 out of a possible 300.

recruit climbs a wooden wall at Leatherneck Square, which is filled with many physically and mentally challenging obstacles.

Opposite page: Recruits move quickly through an obstacle at Leatherneck Square on Parris Island, along with countless hours of physical conditioning. Recruits leave boot camp in the best physical shape of their lives, and the Marine drill instructors have instilled a healthy lifestyle that the recruits will carry with them for the rest of their Marine careers.

Above: "One for the Corps," a drill instructor yells to a recruit, as he tries to pump one more repetition out at Leatherneck Square. Optimal physical condition is strongly stressed while recruits receive sixty hours of instruction from the drill instructors.

Recruits train for countless hours on hand-to-hand combat to include punches, holds, throws, kicks, and a variety of blows to the body. The Marine Corps Martial Arts Program (MCMAP) program consists of instruction in various martial arts styles.

commissions that were offered to him to remain an enlisted sergeant. In his words, "I'd rather be an outstanding sergeant than just another officer."

You Don't Join the Marines. You Become One.

It was only in January 2005 that the Marines' unprecedented streak of 122 consecutive months of meeting their recruiting mission was broken. Every Marine recruiter had averaged two and a half new recruits per month for well over a decade, for a total of more than forty thousand per year. Long known as

Recruits are doing things they thought would be impossible, like commando-crawling twenty feet through a puddle of water and not missing a beat. Obstacles help build confidence, strength, agility, teamwork, and a sense of self-accomplishment.

recruit moves across a rope obstacle at Leatherneck Square and looks for the end point, where he gets off the rope and reports to the drill instructor overseeing this obstacle. He then asks the drill instructor for permission to move on. Usually the recruit will have to recite a general order or answer a Marine history question before receiving such permission. If the recruit responds incorrectly, he will negotiate the obstacle again.

innovators on the battlefield, the Marines' success in recruiting was due in part to some nontraditional means of recruitment. For example, Corps recruiters could be found at concerts and festivals, as well as the X-Games for a couple of years in the late 1990s. They knew early on that just setting up a table in the halls of the local high schools wasn't going to be enough.

Once a young man or woman signs a contract to enlist, he or she is in limbo between the civilian world and military service. During this time, they're all known as "poolees." Depending on when they sign, some may be poolees for only a few weeks, while others may hold the status for upwards of a year. At this point in the process, recruiters remain in constant

recruits receive instruction in the Marine Corps Martial Arts Program (MCMAP) during week four of their training.

Battlefields and countries where Marines have paid the ultimate sacrifice for God and country include Belleau Wood, Guadalcanal, Tarawa, Peleliu, Chosin Reservoir, Somalia, Afghanistan, and Iraq.

At the rifle range, a recruit becomes the deadliest weapon on battlefields around the world. Marines have been rifle marksmanship masters throughout their history, having defeated overwhelming odds with deadly accurate rifle fire. Recruits fire on targets during week seven of their training. No matter what job a Marine has after completing recruit training, all Marines are riflemen first.

Opposite page: Recruits become familiar with the M16A2 service rifle. Week seven is firing week at the rifle range, which includes prequalification and rifle qualification day.

Above: During week ten, recruits train for war during the Crucible, as "causalities" are taken during an exercise. The recruits must pick up the wounded and take them to a casualty collection point off the battlefield. Teamwork and communication are needed to move several bodies from the "kill zone."

For the recruit, the Crucible is the true test of mental and physical endurance. The continuous fifty-four-hour rite of passage for all Marines involves completion of various obstacles while being subjected to food and sleep deprivation.

contact with them. This may be the time that a slightly overweight poolee is working to shed some pounds before reporting to training. Or, the poolee may not have finished high school yet, and the recruiter is continually stressing the importance of hard work and studying. The actions and commitment of the poolees often indicate how well they will perform during training and in their time of service.

While some recruits still arrive at Parris Island or in San Diego under duress, the majority sign on in eager anticipation of becoming one of the few, the proud. Talk to any recruiter or recruit and he or she will tell you that if you want to join the military, there are always the other branches. But if you want to become somebody with purpose, direction, discipline, and honor, there is only the Marine Corps.

Each year, the U.S. government commissions a study of American youth to determine their attitudes about military service. Year in and year out some results stay the same: notably, that the Marine Corps is the most elite among all the forces. Why is this? Is it the esprit de corps that's evident whenever two or more Marines gather? Is it their refusal to back down to any foe? Is it their razor-sharp dress blue uniforms? Yes, yes, and yes; it's all of them. So it should come as no surprise that those who are more prone to choose enlistment over college or the job force after high school naturally lean toward the Marines.

Initiation

Recruits who walked with their heads high and chests out for weeks before leaving home arrive in the middle of the night at either Parris Island or San Diego with little of that confidence intact. They've all heard the legends of drill instructors, and they know enough to remain silent when they arrive. The first

Opposite page: During the Crucible, recruits low-crawl in mud and water as loud machine gun and artillery fire rings through the woods. Recruits are stressed, hungry, tired, and pushed to physical exhaustion. When incoming rounds sound, all recruits must take cover or stop crawling.

night of training is pure sensory overload: Drill instructors (DI) shouting at you to get off their bus, a one-sided fifteen-second phone call home, a very thorough haircut, and USMC-issued everything are the highlights. The paperwork and processing drag on forever. It's truly the night that won't end, since recruits often don't sleep at all until the end of the next day. But if they can withstand the shouts of the DIs, their own self-doubt, and the occasional scorn of their fellow recruits, the end result of their training can be described as nothing less than a transformation. In fact, during tearful family reunions it's not uncommon for a new Marine to have to introduce himself to his family because he's not the same person he was when he left home.

Indoctrination

The thirteen weeks of training are hell on earth for most recruits, a little less so for others. In each platoon a few recruits always stand above the others. They are the born leaders—the cream of the crop that the Corps relies on. These recruits are able to make decisions and remain calm, and in so doing inspire other recruits to follow them. It's not that the DIs go easier on these recruits; in fact, it's just the opposite. The reasoning is that it gives these leaders more opportunities to serve as examples for the others. Eventually, even the weakest recruit will step up and take the leaders' place on the quarterdeck for a little incentive training. Teamwork is the essence of life in the Corps, and the drill instructors have many time-proven ways to foster its development.

Recruits charge with fixed bayonets in a photo that is reminiscent of a memorable page in Marine Corps history, when men from B Company, 1/26 charged a North Vietnamese position outside the firebase of Khe Sanh on March 30, 1968. The Marines attacked the position to recover the bodies of fallen brothers from an ambush by the enemy the night before. They recovered the bodies and killed many North Vietnamese soldiers in the process.

The schedule for recruit training activities, like everything else, appears to the recruits to be random and without planning. They are not told anything until it is deemed necessary for them to be in the know. But there are reasons why one exercise may be a mile from the next. For one, it provides the drill instructors with extra time to get in a little drill instruction. DIs never miss an opportunity to instill discipline and respect for the Corps' past through drilling practice. The back-and-forth nature of crisscrossing the training depot between exercises also has the effect of creating disorder for the recruits. And that creates confusion, which in turn causes the recruits to turn to one another for a collective sense of understanding. It's the only option they have.

Again, it is this teamwork that all DIs try to instill in the recruits. Adversity hits each recruit in different ways during training, which causes one of two reactions. Either the recruit quits, or more often than not, he or she understands that it's impossible to get through recruit training alone. Thus, it's impossible to serve in the Corps alone. This is not, after all, a Marine Corps of one.

The Crucible

Recruits know the end of training is near when they embark upon the Crucible. Since 1996, when it became a part of recruit training, the Crucible has become the defining moment for many soon-to-be Marines. This fifty-four-hour ordeal is an all-out assault on the mind and body of each participant. With only four hours of sleep and a ration of two meals, ready to eat (MREs) per recruit, the rest of the time is spent in team-building exercises and physical or mental tests. Finally, when they can take no more, the only thing that stands between them and a warrior's breakfast of all-you-can-eat steak, eggs, and potatoes is a forced ten-mile hike. That's typical Marine Corps style.

After another week of mostly drilling, drilling, and more drilling, the recruits look almost completely like Marines. There is little left of the person who showed up on the bus several weeks earlier, figuratively and physically. In an emotional ceremony with family they haven't seen in months looking on, recruits obtain the title "Marine" during the emblem ceremony.

This is when they receive the coveted eagle, globe, and anchor, the symbol of the Corps that they will forever wear on their covers and their hearts. The next day is graduation, after which, it should come as no surprise, the nation's newest Marines waste no time in departing the training depot.

At the conclusion of their training, they are all basically trained Marines. Many parents fear that at this point their son or daughter will be shipped off to the Middle East to fight. In fact, the next place they'll report to will be the specialty school for their assigned military operational specialty (MOS) for extended and thorough skills training. For example, the School of Infantry is a seven-and-a-half-week period of training at Camp Lejeune, North Carolina. The Marines have always extolled the virtues of their training and the expertise it creates. Their record of success leaves little doubt that they are right.

Officer Candidates School (OCS)

There is a saying among the Marines at Marine Corps Recruiting Command: "Big E, Little O." Basically, the great majority of their recruiting efforts focus on the forty thousand enlisted recruits—Big E—they require each year, as opposed to the two thousand officer candidates—Little O—they need. The Marines are known to turn away officer candidates. Referred to in *Inc.* magazine (April 1998) as the best management training program in America, it's no surprise that spots at OCS are as coveted as they are. The primary difference between recruit training and OCS is that for recruits it's a screening period of sorts, whereas for officer candidates, it's all about becoming a leader of leaders, as the recruiting materials say. They are screened long before they get to Quantico, Virginia, for their journey into the officers' ranks of the Corps. But make no mistake, that journey is no cakewalk. It is well known

The Marine Corps offers an opportunity for young people to learn and teach leadership and teamwork and develop a strong moral foundation that will stay with a Marine for the rest of his or her life.

The Marine Corps is rich with tradition—Marines are masters of drill and ceremony. The precision of their movements is drilled repeatedly for weeks.

throughout Marines of all ranks that enlisted training is practically a day at the beach compared to what the officer candidates endure. But in the end it's this understanding that serves officers well on the battlefield when issuing orders to those in their command. It's one way a twenty-two-year-old lieutenant in his first tour garners the respect of a thirty-five-year-old gunnery sergeant with seventeen years of service under his belt.

Since the Corps' inception on November 10, 1775, at the Tun Tavern in Philadelphia, Marines have grown accustomed to the role of underdog. No matter the forum, the Marines have been outnumbered, whether on the battlefield practically any time they fight or in the halls of our own government, and they never miss an opportunity to turn the tables. Outnumbered and surrounded at the Chosin Reservoir, the Marines executed perhaps the most valiant fighting extraction ever carried out, leaving no man behind, while inflicting massive casualties on the enemy. Likewise, before the Senate Committee on Naval Affairs in 1946, General Alexander A. Vandegrift, the eighteenth commandant of the Marine Corps, delivered a passionate speech that defended the Corps based on past accomplishments and current capabilities. But he stopped short of begging for its continued existence. He concluded his speech by saying, "We have pride in ourselves and in our past, but we do not rest our case on any presumed ground of gratitude owing us from the nation. The bended knee is not a tradition of our Corps." An understatement, to say the least.

Drill instructors lead each of their platoons as they pass in review before the headquarters element, command staff, and VIPs.

Chapter 2

WINNING STARTS BEFORE THE WAR

STRUCTURE AND PLANNING OF THE MARINE CORPS

Ask the general public what the Marines train for and you'll probably get an answer along the lines of "to fight wars." Ask a Marine the same question and the answer you get will be "to win wars." Semantics? Hardly. To the Marine Corps there's a huge difference.

The Marine Corps is America's force in readiness, but you have to dig a little deeper to understand what that actually means. Each branch of the military has a specialty. The Navy, like the Marines, projects power from the sea; however, it does so with long-range Tomahawk missiles from as far as a thousand miles away. The air force defends the United States and protects its interests through air and space power. The army maintains a large ground force that is primarily responsible for land-based military operations.

There's only one drawback to having large forces capable of doing all these things: None of them can do their job quickly. It takes weeks for naval ships to reach their destination. It takes just as long for the army to assemble its forces. And, while the air force may have the air assets to reach any point in the world within a matter of hours, it doesn't have a sufficient ground force to get close enough to an enemy to call down fire.

The Marine Corps has capabilities similar to all three larger branches. With a force of only two hundred thousand or so Marines, the Corps' expertise across all three arenas of war makes it the smallest combined force in the world, but also the most deadly. The ability to project massive amounts of power ashore, whether by amphibious landing vehicles or transport helicopters, or both at the same time, sets the

The highly maneuverable and heavily armed Apache helicopters fly over Iraq in support of ground combat operations. The AH-64 Apache is the world's premier attack helicopter and was designed to withstand harsh environmental conditions and the stress of combat.

Opposite page: An American flag that was once flown over Ground Zero in New York City is prepared for a ceremony in the city of Fallujah, Iraq, to remember those who lost their lives in the events on September 11, 2001, and those service members who sacrificed their lives to bring justice to the people responsible.

Marines rush toward a building during the initial actions of the 15th Marine Expeditionary Unit (Special Operations Capable) in Iraq.

Marines of Company B, 1st Battalion, 8th Marine Regiment, Regimental Combat Team 7, fire a mortar round at the enemies' position in Fallujah, Iraq, during Operation Al Fajr. This was an offensive operation to eradicate enemy forces within the city of Fallujah in support of continuing security and stabilization operations in the Al Anbar Province of Iraq by units of the 1st Marine Division.

Lance Corporal Michael T. Hebert, with Lima Company, 3rd Battalion, 1st Marine Regiment, holds his rifle. Hebert was deployed to Iraq in support of Operation Iraqi Freedom.

a significant aspect of preparing for war is the willingness to throw all plans out the window should events on the battlefield call for it.

Careful planning and execution begin in training. Marines train relentlessly, whether during peacetime or the months leading up to a deployment, just so they will be able to act on instinct the moment the chips are down and action becomes necessary. One critical aspect of this training is the element of surprise, and not the type of surprise that involves them sneaking up on an unsuspecting enemy patrol in the middle of the night. Rather, the surprises are the problems, malfunctions, and distractions that get thrown into training exercises when the Marines least expect them. Marines will tell you that as soon as a training exercise is going along smoothly, the officer in charge will throw an unexpected wrench into the works. And, sometimes, they'll just pile them on. After all, conditions on the battlefield practically sprint toward chaos and disorder. The end result of one action may not always be what's expected. Sometimes this is good and sometimes it's very, very bad. So even if you can't prepare for every possible situation, you can at least learn to remain calm and in control of the situation. And that control will only come about when the atmosphere remains flexible.

The very nature of battle keeps events on the battlefield from following a logical path. But they do shape one another; cause and effect play a great role in the fluidity of war. So it's not as much about training as you would with a rifle or a tank, although certainly that aspect is very important, but training exercises in the Corps often take turns meant to hone instincts.

For officers, it starts in the Basic School after their initial training at OCS. New lieutenants are briefed in the classroom for the exercises they are about to carry out. They're given objectives and the opportunity to plan and map out their course. But almost no sooner than they've set foot on the simulated battlefield, commanding officers start to mix things up. They purposely add friction to the situation to test the younger officers' ability to hold up under uncertain circumstances.

Major Ryan Paterson recounted a training experience he was involved with in 1996, early in his career. The difference that day was that Mother Nature was the one adding the friction. Off the coast of Italy, his unit was back-loading tanks

Marines apart. The fact that they can be on any enemy shore within six hours of trouble arising ensures that it'll be a while before any of the other services catch up.

The Marines spend a considerable amount of time analyzing war on all levels, as well as the best way to accomplish their ultimate goal: bending an enemy to their will. War is a social process involving the violent interaction of two groups or countries, and social events can be shaped. So it would make sense for the Marines to believe they can absolutely affect the outcome of a war through careful planning and execution. Oddly enough, at the same time, they recognize that

Marines assigned to Bravo Company, 2nd Assault Amphibian Battalion, 2nd Marine Division, use amphibious assault vehicles to block a roadway during Operation Southern Fire. The mission kicked off in the early morning hours of August 25, 2005, with coalition forces sealing off the town of Amiriyah and the settlement known as Ferris Town in Al Anbar Province. It was an effort to establish a permanent presence of Iraqi police and army and to prepare for upcoming elections.

onto transport vehicles. While tanks aren't typically amphibious, they can easily work their way through four to six feet of water. Once on dry land, they have bilge pumps that get rid of any water they may have taken on while coming ashore.

That day, the weather was getting progressively worse. As the Marines were moving one of the tanks into position in the surf, an exceptionally large wave broadsided and swamped the tank with the driver inside. With no time to decide on a plan of action, the Marines did what they do best: they trusted their instincts. As the driver's compartment was filling with water, a tank driver on the beach wasted no time

in moving his tank into position to tow the disabled tank to safety. Guys were diving in the water doing everything they could to attach cables in any way possible to the tank to get it and their fellow Marine towed to safety.

These same Marines had spent some time planning for a tank rescue. But as Major Paterson is quick to point out, the Marines don't train to re-create specific incidents, they train to make their minds work. When you have no choice but to come up with a solution, you're much more likely to trust your ability to do so when the opportunity to do it again comes up.

That day in Italy ended successfully. The tank, the driver, and all involved came out unscathed. That night, it became a story to laugh about. But if it weren't for the fast thinking of a few Marines who wouldn't know any other way to approach an emergency but to simply react, it may have been a very different ending.

Marines are well known for more than their ferociousness in battle. Having studied their own successes and failures for over two hundred years, they strive for a certain level of creativity as well. Each Marine must be able to fully appreciate the gravity of any combat situation in which he or she finds himself. The leaders among them must be able to think their way through it all. Practical solutions to improbable sit-

Pictured third from right firing the M198 howitzer, Lance Corporal Jon E. Bonnell, field artillery cannon crewman, assigned to Bravo Battery, 1st Battalion, 11th Regiment, 2nd Marine Division, and the rest of his crewmembers engage enemy targets during a fire-support mission.

Explosives are detonated in Iraq by Marines conducting combat patrols to find and kill terrorists.

With sunset in Baghdad, enemy activity increases, and Marines exchange small-arms fire with insurgents working in the city. Many of these terrorists are thought to infiltrate Iraq through Syria and Iran.

uations are the Marines' bread and butter. They've built a reputation on them, and it hasn't been by accident.

No matter the scope of the operation, the level of readiness has to be the same. Things can go wrong in an overnight mission just as quickly as they do on a six-month tour. Bullets and missiles don't care if you weren't actually planning to engage an enemy, because when you get right down to it, in war, there's no offense or defense. Each side maintains both roles simultaneously. And any advantage gained can be lost in the blink of an eye.

This level of uncertainty is precisely what makes the human dimension of war so important. Everybody reacts to the violence and improbability of combat differently. Something that may demoralize one person may serve to strengthen another. Because each individual has a unique response, there's no way to predict when fear may take hold.

But there is no doubt that it will. Fear is a reaction to danger and there's no more dangerous place than a battlefield. It's a or nothing, but everyone's in it together, which is exactly wh the Corps stresses the importance of courage. Marines ar fiercely loyal to one another and their Corps. Not one amon them is willing to shame the proud past of his or her "family and there's no way one Marine will let another Marine down Thus, the courage that has become synonymous with th Corps stems directly from the cohesion and sense of team work that's drilled into the Marines from the minute they ge off the bus at boot camp.

The Marine Corps' Mission

Going over enemy shorelines and winning battles. Simpl stated, that's the mission of the Marine Corps. How they g bout it is unique among all other military forces in the world. The Marines have always been an expeditionary force, but only since the mid-1980s have they begun to refer to themselves as such. They have developed a war-fighting doctrine that serves to explain and exploit the natural capabilities of their organization. It is a unifying document among Marines, as it establishes how the Corps thinks about war, as well as combat leadership. Equally as important is the discussion of a common language for ease of communications during chaotic battles.

The expeditionary nature of Corps operations makes it easy to see why Marines are referred to as the tip of the spear in battle and use phrases such as "first in, first out." When trouble arises, it's the Marines who are called to handle it. They can insert themselves over a shoreline or be dropped off en masse by helicopter. More than an expeditionary force, the Marines have the ability to sustain themselves for several weeks at a time, as well. However they arrive, they bring everything they need with them. And they'll make a special point to tell you that they take it all back out with them. They call it "packing their trash," and it's a point of great pride.

Interestingly, when the Cold War ended and nuclear subs became a nonthreat overnight, the focus immediately moved inland, which dramatically increased the role of the Marines. Once the littoral, or coastal, zones of Asia, the Indian Ocean, and the Middle East became the main areas of concern, the ability to quickly land on these shores and move inland became critical as well. Not surprisingly, expeditionary capabilities are increasingly becoming an area of interest to the other branches as they realize the advantages to be gained.

Marines from 3rd Platoon, Bravo Company, Battalion Landing Team (BLT), 1st Battalion, 6th Marines, kick in a locked door during their hunt for Taliban insurgents and arms caches in Afghanistan's Oruzgan Province. BLT 1/6 is the ground combat element of the 22nd Marine Expeditionary Unit (Special Operations Capable).

Still holding his 9mm Beretta, a seriously injured First Sergeant Brad Kasal is helped from a Fallujah house after killing several Iraqi insurgents while shielding a fellow Marine from a grenade blast with his own body.

Marine Air Ground Task Force (MAGTF)

The Marine Corps is miniscule in number when compared to the army, navy, and air force. Yet it would require troops from all three to carry out any mission the Corps is called for. It is an expeditionary force that displays expertise across all three critical areas of warfare: air, land, and sea. While their numbers prevent them from acting as an occupying force in captured enemy territory, Marines are quick to tell you that's not their job. They have the capability to strike quickly, seize an objective, and hold it long enough for the army to come in and take over the occupation. However, recent engagement have stretched out for longer periods of time and Marine have found themselves in the role of a more traditiona ground force. Still, a common comparison pointed out by th Corps is that asking the Marines to be an occupying force i like asking an ambulance to function as a hospital. T understand the methods employed so successfully by th Corps during times of war, you must first understand thei organization and its structure.

For over a half century, the basic construct of Marines a war has involved troops working together from the land, ai and sea. It's known as a Marine air ground task force, or MAGTF, pronounced "mag-taf." The structure of a MAGTF changes with each deployment, but its capabilities never do. The cohesion that a MAGTF offers is off the charts, since all involved are Marines and thus speak the same language, attend the same training courses, and share the same commitment to their Corps. The concept of the MAGTF is scalable, and there are three different sizes in which they operate, depending on the scope of the mission they set out to accomplish. From smallest to largest, they are the Marine expeditionary unit, the Marine expeditionary brigade, and the Marine expeditionary force. And regardless of each Marine's individual role within the combat structure, any operation will be commanded by a senior officer, usually a colonel to a lieutenant general.

Marine Expeditionary Unit (MEU)

The smallest MAGTF arrangement is the battalion-size Marine expeditionary unit (MEU), which is small enough to act as an independent force or as part of a joint task force. An

Marines check for insurgents by going door to door in Iraq. Bolt cutters and battering rams are used to breach doors and gates, but sometimes the foot method works just as well.

During a service at Camp Korean Village, Iraq, thirty-four helmets and rifles stand as a memorial for fallen Marines and sailors of the 31st Marine Expeditionary Unit and Marine Heavy Helicopter Squadron 361.

MEU consists of four distinct elements. The command element (CE), which serves as headquarters, is headed up by a single officer, usually a colonel. The ground combat element (GCE) is a battalion landing team, which is an infantry battalion reinforced with tanks, artillery, combat engineers, amphibious vehicles, light armored vehicles, and other ground combat assets. The aviation combat element (ACE) is made up of a composite squadron of both fixed aircraft (airplanes) and rotary-wing aircraft (helicopters). The combat service support element (CSSE) consists of an MEU service support group that handles all logistics and administrative needs. The Marines prefer not to travel with more personnel or equipment than necessary, and thus the exact arrangement of these elements can be customized based upon the task at hand. Additional artillery, armor, or air units can always be attached.

The MEU may also be classified as special operations capable (SOC). This program was formed in the late 1980s, in part because of shortcomings brought to light by the October 1983 disaster in Beirut that left two hundred Marines dead after an Iranian drove a nineteen-ton truck bomb into their barracks. In keeping with Marine Corps tradition, there was no push to train a separate special operations force within the Corps, such as the army's green berets or the navy SEALs. The Marines believe they already have the world's most elite warriors, so all they need to do is complete special training prior to their deployment to be classified as SOC. Rather than selecting a few Marines from the ranks, all four elements of an MEU work relentlessly during their buildup before deployment to become cleared as SOC. Additional training maneuvers to do so require more time away from family and ceaseless hours of work. And much like people who have known each other for years will joke that they can finish each other's sentences, this additional training bonds the Marines so tightly that they can practically finish the others' radio transmissions should they find themselves in the heat of battle. But the end result is force that can artfully execute any one of twenty-three missions within six hours of an alert. Since the Marine Corps doesn't actually participate in the United States Special Operations Command (USSOCOM) organization, they are able to act much more expeditiously when necessary.

The MEU (SOC) is by far the most compact, responsive, and capable military unit in the world. Each MEU (SOC) has multiple means to take troops and equipment to practically any type of fight from well over the horizon. And once the ball is rolling on an operation, they have no need for external support for at least fifteen days.

Typically, there are three MEUs assigned to each of the U.S. Navy Atlantic and Pacific Fleets, and one based on Okinawa. While one MEU is on deployment, another one is training for deployment and one is standing down, resting its Marines who have just returned home.

Marine Expeditionary Brigade (MEB)

A Marine expeditionary brigade (MEB) is larger than an MEU, because it consists of much larger air and support contingencies. The 3rd Marine Expeditionary Brigade is the Marine Corps' only permanently forward-deployed brigade-size MAGTF. Serving as a force in readiness, it is fully capable of rapid deployment and can execute a wide spectrum of orders, including humanitarian assistance, high-intensity combat, disaster relief, and amphibious assault. The Marines of 3rd MEB conduct combined operations and training throughout the Pacific region as well.

Marines with Company B, 1st Battalion, 8th Marine Regiment, Regimental Combat Team 7, watch one another's backs while securing a street corner on November 23, 2004, in Fallujah, Iraq, during Operation Al Fajr.

A scout with 2nd Platoon, 1st LAR, fires on insurgents during Operation Steel Curtain. A sentry spotted masked men moving in houses across from the platoon. The men were providing security for a massive improvised explosive device underneath a bridge. *Corporal Ken Melton*

Marine Expeditionary Force (MEF)

A Marine expeditionary force (MEF) is comprised of a Marine division with an artillery regiment, several tank battalions, several light armored vehicle (LAV) battalions, as well as an air wing. Each division consists of thirty-eight thousand Marines, including their supporting air wing and logistical support group.

The Marine Corps consists of three such active-duty divisions, with each one designated as either amphibious or expeditionary. The divisions are entirely too large to be rapidly deployed, so the Corps sends them out in MEBs consisting of roughly sixteen thousand Marines. The 1st and 2nd Marine Divisions focus on the amphibious mission and provide the personnel for each two-thousand-man forward-deployed MEU. The two divisions share responsibility to maintain an MEU trained battalion task force on Okinawa, Japan. In major wars, such as the Persian Gulf War, the divisions will collectively depart on all available amphibious ships. That particular war ultimately consisted of the 1st and 2nd Marine Divisions with an artillery regiment, several tank and LAV battalions, as well as considerable Marine air and support units.

The building, where several of the masked men were hiding, goes up in flames after being hit by HE rounds during the firefight with 2nd Platoon scouts. *Corporal Ken Melton*

Rounds fly as Sergeant Robert E. Canales, chief scout with 2nd Platoon, 1st LAR, fires upon an insurgent position during an hour-long firefight. Canales is a native of San Fernando, California. *Corporal Ken Melton*

Every Marine a Rifleman.
But Most Do Other Things, Too.

No matter the size of the MAGTF, one thing's for sure: infantry Marines will play a big role. A Marine's primary identity as a rifleman is a testament to that major role. While infantry units make up the ground combat element of a MAGTF, there are many different ways in which they can be configured to do so. "Ground combat element" is a bit of a misnomer, since these Marines spend a lot of time onboard navy ships. But when they're called by the country to carry out a mission, they're right where they need to be.

Whether they are to cross over enemy shorelines by sea or by helicopter, infantry Marines will depart from one of the navy's ships. They will all have their rifles, and they will always be on the alert. While all Marines are riflemen, there is also an actual infantry military occupational specialty (MOS) titled rifleman. These Marines are the foundation of the ground combat element. They are the heart of the fire team in the rifle squad and the foundation of the scout team

in the Light Armored Reconnaissance (LAR) squad. Riflemen are more than simple foot soldiers; they are a MAGTF's primary scout, assault, and close-combat force. Their weapons are the M16A2, M203 grenade launcher, and the squad automatic weapon (SAW).

While Marines have a great deal of weapons at their disposal, using them properly takes specialized training. A machine gunner will provide direct fire support with the 7.62mm medium machine gun, the .50-caliber machine gun, and the 40mm heavy machine gun. Mortarmen employ the 60mm light mortar and the 81mm medium mortar to supply indirect fire. The TOW-2 heavy antitank and antivehicle weapon system is expertly handled by missilemen. Antibunker and antiarmor fire is provided by infantry assaultmen with the shoulder-launched multipurpose assault weapon (SMAW), the Dragon medium assault antitank weapon, and Javelin medium assault antitank weapon.

No matter the mission these men are assigned, they have to first reach their primary objective. If their goal is just over

the shoreline, they will arrive by amphibious assault vehicle. If the target zone is a few hundred miles inland, they'll be delivered by a troop transport helicopter such as a CH-46 Sea Knight transport helicopter, or more likely they and some of their artillery equipment will arrive in a CH-53E Super Stallion helicopter and cover any remaining distance on foot. Just as the individual roles of infantrymen are varied and unique, so are the men and women who make up an amphibious crew or a flight crew. One primary difference is the presence of women in the flight crew. While government regulations prevent women from most battle-related MOSs,

An Iraqi citizen lifts his arms to be checked by a Marine using an optic sight for weapons or other objects before entering a polling site. Lance Corporal Steven R. Ybarra and other Marines with 3rd Battalion, 1st Marine Regiment, assist Iraqi Security Forces by providing security for these elections as more than three hundred citizens cast their vote.

Scouts with 2nd Platoon, 1st LAR, conduct house searches as part of Operation Steel Curtain. The scouts would later find a booby-trapped house during their patrol. *Corporal Ken Melton*

Marines from Company I, 3rd Battalion, 25th Marines uncovered boxes of ammunition, explosives, electronic equipment, and propaganda during a cache find on a patrol.

they are allowed to serve as pilots and naval flight officers (navigators), and they do so quite capably.

An amphibious crew's primary task is to deliver ground troops safely from a ship over the horizon to the enemy shoreline. This involves more than simply taking the wheel and heading out full speed ahead for the beach. These Marines put in long hours before they even leave the boat to ensure that everything's in place. Once onboard the assault vehicle, the crew assumes control, handling everything from operation and maintenance to identifying and engaging targets with precise fire from weapons systems such as the Mk.19 40mm automatic grenade launcher, the .50-caliber M2 machine gun, and the 5.56mm Mk.46 light machine gun.

Transporting Marines in the air takes more personnel than getting them somewhere over the water. A transport helicopter like the CH-53E requires enlisted Marines to load equipment, operate communication equipment, and perform navigational duties. Then there are the naval flight officers

who assist in the operation of the helicopter itself, direct supporting fire for ground forces, and also update ground force commanders with aerial intelligence. And, of course, there are the pilots who carry out observation, troop and equipment transport, rescue, utility, and fire-suppression missions.

Maintaining a self-sustaining force requires more than ground combat and airmobile troops. Marines of the combat service support element make significant contributions to the MAGTF. They are the ones who keep the vehicles supplied with fuel and their fellow Marines supplied with food. Combat service support specialists help out with loading and unloading personnel, equipment, and supplies aboard ships, and other troop transport. And you can't have people jumping out of planes or equipment falling from the sky without properly packed parachutes. That's exactly what parachute riggers do. Assault vehicles are only a small fraction of the motor vehicles operated by the Marine Corps. The support crews drive the rest to assist in land-based transportation of Marines

A wounded Marine is transported from one medical ward to another for further treatment.

and equipment. And when those vehicles break down, there are Marine mechanics to get them up and running again. It's easy to think about support operations taking place well behind the front lines of battle, but mechanics are a good example of how support operations have to take place where the problems are at times. It's one thing to pull a car or truck into a garage, put it up on a rack, take your time figuring out what's wrong, and then fix it. It's something else all together when you have to get out to the middle of a battlefield and do it all while bullets are flying and missiles are dropping.

With a captured insurgent's RPK machine gun tucked into the straps of his pack, a Marine from Battalion Landing Team 1st Battalion, 2nd Marines—the ground combat element of the 22nd Marine Expeditionary Unit (Special Operations Capable)—waits to board a seven-ton truck after Operation Moon River in Kubaysah, Iraq, on December 31, 2005. Operation Moon River is part of an ongoing counterinsurgency effort by the 22nd MEU (SOC) in Iraq's Al Anbar province, undertaken as part of Operation Iraqi Freedom. *Gunnery Sergeant Keith A. Milks*

A Marine from Battalion Landing Team 1st Battalion, 2nd Marines, 22nd MEU (SOC), provides security on patrol through Kubaysah during Operation Moon River. *Sergeant Robert A. Sturkie*

Three Interrelated Levels of War

The USMC doctrinal manual titled *Warfighting* goes into some detail about the levels of war and the pecking order they fall into. Top to bottom, the levels of war are strategic, operational, and tactical.

Military strategy is at the top of this list because it's about planning wars. Strategy defines goals. It decides who will go where and what equipment they'll take with them. And it determines exactly how, and under what conditions, force will be used in battle. Strategy is the result of specific political and policy objectives. As such, Marines regard it as the foundation of authority for any operation in which they're called to serve.

On the list, the tactical level is last. For purposes of clarity in discussion, here it comes second, just as it does in

As small-arms fire echoes through the city of Kubaysah during Operation Moon River, Marines from 22nd MEU (SOC) take cover and scan rooftops and alleyways for possible threats. *Gunnery Sergeant Keith A. Milks*

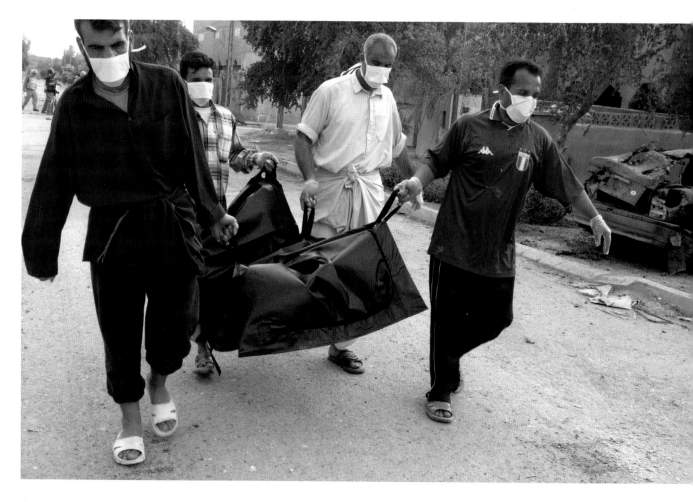

Local Iraqis pick up dead insurgents in and around Fallujah during breaks in the fighting.

Warfighting. Tactics are the methods that commanders employ to accomplish the mission with which they've been tasked, whether it's combat related or otherwise. The difference between tactics and strategy is a matter of scope; whereas strategy is about winning wars, tactics are about winning battles. In a combat situation, this would involve how firepower is used and how each success is built upon to defeat the enemy. In a noncombat scenario, a commander would recommend whatever tactics are necessary to accomplish missions such as maintaining order and providing security.

Finally, the operational level bridges the gaps between strategy and tactics. It is at this level that decisions are made regarding when and where an enemy will be met. Not as broad in scope as strategy or narrow in focus as tactics, success at the operational level involves knowing when to fight and when to hold out for a better opportunity. It's easy to see how these levels can overlap. No situation will ever fall clearly into only one category; thus, commanders exercise judgment with caution. All too easily, circumstances can shift and take any positive momentum with them.

The ultimate goal of war is to bend an enemy to your will. Whichever side of the fight controls the initiative is more likely to come out on top. Recognizing how easily the sands of happenstance can shift, the Marines are careful not to make any distinctions between who's assaulting whom. The fact is that once a skirmish begins, both sides do so with great passion.

For example, the majority of the fighting that took place in Iraq in late 2005 was the result of insurgencies with enough troop strength to stage an ambush or an outright fight. These insurgents rarely, if ever, fought in broad daylight. They preferred to take cover within vacant homes, alleys, even holy places such as mosques. When Marines went out on patrol within the villages of Iraq known to hold insurgents, they expected to take fire. From that standpoint, they were on the

During Operation Liberty Express III (December 11–18, 2005), Private First Class Matthew P. Henderson guards an entry point to Haditha City, Iraq. Henderson is an M240G medium machine gunner with Security Company, Combat Logistics Battalion 2, 2nd Marine Logistics Group (Forward). Over forty of his fellow Marines took part in the operation. *Lance Corporal Joel Abshier*

defensive. However, they were more than ready to return fire, and that placed them squarely on the offensive.

Accomplishing the Mission

Marines, past and present, young and old, know only one way to go about the task at hand: Don't stop until the battle's won. From day one of recruit training, Marines learn the value of teamwork, and it's a lesson they take with them into combat. With the rock-hard will of each individual Marine melded together, they make for an imposing and driven force that will accept nothing less than victory.

Project Maximum Force

You hear the phrase a lot in regard to Marines: Project maximum force ashore. What does that mean exactly? From their

Two Marines with Company L, 3rd Battalion, 7th Marine Regiment, stand guard in Ar Ramadi, Iraq, during Operation Shank on December 3, 2005. *Corporal Shane Suzuki*

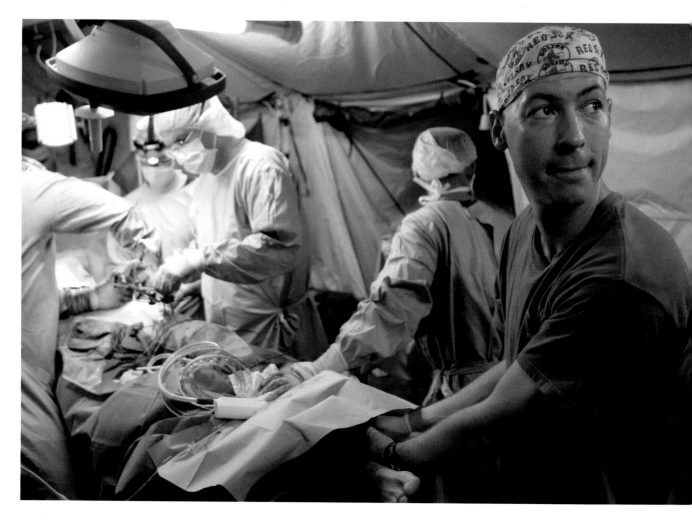

Medical personnel operate on a Marine wounded in combat operations in Fallujah.

humble beginnings as ship security personnel until now, the Marines have been known for two things: their marksmanship and their beach landings. The latter is where all the talk of projecting power comes from. In much earlier times, Marines would either wade or row themselves ashore in what amounted to lifeboats from the navy's ships. They now have the capability to roll in like thunder from over the horizon in any number of ways. They can arrive by helicopter, or they may rumble ashore in armored assault vehicles (AAVs), or they may land in a conventional landing craft, air cushioned (LCAC). Worst of all for the enemy, Marines may arrive in all three simultaneously. Or they could thump three different locations all at the same time. You can see how the combinations of scenarios can practically paralyze an enemy before anything even gets started.

To add another element of confusion to the mix for an enemy, any strike that does happen is likely to happen at night. Not only does the darkness provide extra cover, but it allows Marines to capitalize on the advantages of their technology over that of the enemy in most cases. Night-vision equipment is practically standard for all Marines. During the day, their only advantage is their training.

This is one reason why the Marine Corps Martial Arts Program (MCMAP) was developed. The leadership of the Corps rightly assumed that urban and police-type peacekeeping missions would become prevalent in the twenty-first century. This being the case, they wanted to make sure that Marines had every weapon possible at their disposal, whether it's their hands, their mind, or their rifle. They walk with confidence and they fight with pride. It's just one example of why the ethos of the Marine Corps has nothing to do with technology; rather, it's all about the Marine with a rifle and how he handles it in the face of an enemy.

Captain Rory Quinn, commanding officer of Company L, 3rd Battalion, 7th Marine Regiment, takes cover near an abandoned building in Ar Ramadi, Iraq, during Operation Block Party 6 on November 30, 2005. *Corporal Shane Suzuki*

Most of us think of the Marine Corps as solely a light ground force: infantry formations without all the heavy armored forces the army is laden with. For the most part, this is true, but the Corps also operates its own air force. It just happens to be the fifth-largest air force in the world. And its primary mission is to support the troops on the ground, whether the mission is getting the Marines safely to their destination or providing the firepower called in by the ground troops.

To call communications between Marines on the ground and in the air "tight" is an understatement. In fact, all operations, including aviation, are almost exclusively directed from the ground. Because the Marine Corps is an expeditionary force with the mission of penetrating the enemy's defenses and securing territory, the aviators that fly with them do so in support of the ground mission. While this may sound like the pilots take a back seat to the action, rest assured there is nothing boring about flying Mach 1 at five hundred feet off the ground. The Marines call this close-air support, and it is just one of the three major tactical innovations in modern ground combat that the Marines can take credit for. There have only been five in total.

Beach Landings Then and Now

Another method with which the Marines have redefined modern ground combat is amphibious assault. It's been the calling card of the Marines for over two centuries. As America's expeditionary force, the Corps has worked long and hard to perfect its mission of going over enemy shores and winning battles. Indeed, some of the most famous moments in the Marines' storied history have come on beaches in far-off lands, none more so than Iwo Jima. But technological advancements and techniques like airmobile assault have moved many "beach landings" several hundred miles inland. In fact, using helicopters to insert troops into combat situations, or even behind enemy lines, is yet another way the Marines redefined warfare in the twentieth century. The techniques involved in airmobile assault are full of advantages, the most important of which is that Marines aren't left exposed as

Marines on a night raid prepare to breach a door into what locals said could be an insurgent stronghold or bomb-making location.

easy targets for enemy fire while floating on a breeze and a parachute. They're delivered straight to the ground where they can fan out in a practiced formation, providing cover for one another, and head directly toward their objective.

When the Corps does need to take a beach front, they can do so in any number of ways. This is a good place to revisit the difference between tactics and techniques. Landing an expeditionary force on an enemy shore to gain a quick-strike advantage is a military technique. But it's not accomplished in the exact same manner each time. Commanding officers must pay close attention to factors such as tides, weather, the number of enemy forces, where they're positioned, and how well they're armed. All of these factors play a role in the decision of which tactics are right for a successful operation. Regardless of the decision, Marine expeditionary units train and prefer to strike at night, as the cover of darkness affords Marines the opportunity to improvise further tactics when necessary.

Traditionally, the Marines have relied on the amphibious tractor to get troops in position. Dubbed the "amtrac," it has been the subject of several redesigns, but never for an aesthetic purpose. A very unlikely-looking vehicle, it is nonetheless extremely capable. It must be able to handle rough seas, come ashore in ten-foot surf, and then make its way inland. Of course, speed isn't the only consideration. Given that there are several Marines onboard, the vehicle must also provide for defense.

Until the early 1980s, the vehicle in service was the landing vehicle, tracked (LVT). The last redesign, labeled the LVT-7, was introduced in 1972 and was intended to do it all. Powered on land by a four-hundred-horsepower engine and on water by twin jet pumps, it climbed three-foot obstacles or a 60 percent grade, without tipping over. Likewise, a 40 percent side-slope was no problem, nor was an eight-foot wide gulley. As for defense, an electric turret on top carried

A Marine with Combined Anti-Armor Team White, 3rd Battalion, 7th Marine Regiment, runs to cover in Ar Ramadi during Operation Block Party 6. *Corporal Shane Suzuki*

he reliable M2 .50-caliber heavy machine gun, as well as a thousand rounds of belted ammunition divided into two-hundred-round cans. Additional firepower was provided by a 40mm Mk.19 automatic grenade launcher with ninety-six belted rounds available. The LVT-7's biggest shortcoming was its vulnerability once on shore. A bolt-on armored plate was fashioned for it, but it added several thousand pounds to the weight. Rather than go through another redesign to address the problem, the Corps had loftier goals in mind.

Advanced Amphibious Assault Vehicle (AAAV)

The advanced amphibious assault vehicle (AAAV) is the world's most advanced fighting vehicle. The capabilities of the AAAV are like nothing before it and the stuff of a Marine's dreams. Most impressively, its speed on the water is more than triple that of its predecessor. At a top speed of twenty-five knots (roughly forty-three miles per hour), the

AAAV seemingly skims the surface and enables the ship it launches from to remain completely out of sight of land over the visual horizon and still land onshore within an hour of departing the ship. This is accomplished in part by a high-speed hull that features a retractable bow flap, which acts like a surfboard. And as for power, the AAAV comes up big, with a twenty-six-hundred-horsepower (that's not a typo) tur-bocharged diesel engine that's as functional as it is powerful. Self-contained, it requires an oil change only once every two years (that's also not a typo). The automatic transmission powers twin twenty-three-inch water jets that drive the vehicle to within a few hundred yards of the shoreline. It's at that point that the retractable track system is lowered to take over and get it the rest of the way in. The track system allows the water to flow much more freely under the vehicle than was possible with previous amtrac models, and it can be raised or lowered in less than twenty seconds.

Standing watch on December 13, 2005, at Post One in Hit, Iraq, Lance Corporals Travis Vetterkind (left) and Daniel Kohs are members of Company G, Battalion Landing Team, 2nd Battalion, 1st Marines. The unit is currently executing security and stability operations in the city of Hit, while serving on a Western Pacific deployment with the 13th Marine Expeditionary Unit (Special Operations Capable). *Corporal Andy Hurt*

While armored protection was a shortcoming of the LVT-7, the exact opposite is true for the AAAV. Devised from composite armor, it provides exceptional protection while also keeping the total vehicle weight down to a very manageable level. Armed with an M242 25mm Bushmaster cannon and a 7.62mm machine gun, not only can the AAAV use both weapons from the sea, but it was built to dominate on the battlefield as well.

The Marine Corps is known more for its tactical innovations than its technical developments. Clearly, the AAAV is an exception. Having wisely spent a considerable amount of time and money on its design, the Corps sees no need to replace it anytime soon.

The amphibious capabilities of the current Marine Corps give them access to over 70 percent of the world's shorelines at previously unheard-of speeds. The emergence of airmobile assault techniques has only made the amphibious forces more effective. When an enemy is unsure of whether

they'll be attacked by air, land, or both at the same time, the advantage lies squarely with the Marines.

Innovations in Warfare

We've already discussed three of the biggest innovations that the Marine Corps has contributed to modern warfare: airmobile assault, amphibious assault, and close-air combat support. While these are techniques that have changed the history of war, the Marines have made other contributions now considered essential to military forces around the world, including the thermal boot, individual body armor, and the helicopter. All three were introduced during the Korean conflict. The body armor was a new development that had clear value on the battlefield. Thermal boots and helicopters were brought in to meet specific needs. Korea was where the Corps became proficient in mountain warfare. Being knee-deep in snow with the potential to go down due to frostbite was all the inspiration necessary to develop thermal boots.

Two CH-46s filled with Marines head off to conduct dismounted combat patrols outside Ramadi, Iraq, to sweep the area of insurgents and terrorists.

Rough, mountainous terrain that was barely passable forced the Marines to find another way to transport equipment and troops, which is exactly what they used the helicopters for.

A record of success like the one the Marines boast of doesn't happen by accident. They have fewer personnel than most of the enemy forces they face, yet they carry out one mission after another. Much of their triumph can be attributed to what can only be described as a think tank of sorts. Staffed by the same type of thinkers and doers that have built the legacy of the United States Marine Corps, it's called the Warfighting Laboratory. It is a part of the Marine Corps Combat Development Command and its mission is to improve current and future naval expeditionary warfare capabilities across the spectrum of conflict for current and future forces. In other words: to ensure victory.

Force Recon

A weapon equally as effective as the rifle that Marines carry is the reconnaissance man himself. In addition to basic infantry skills, these guys must also master scout swimming, insertion and extraction techniques, forward observing, photography, and recognition of enemy weapons and equipment. Some are even further trained as static line, free-fall parachutists, and combatant divers.

The USMC Force Recon units are trained to carry out very specialized, small-scale, high-risk operations. Not only do they provide limited raid capabilities, but their scout and patrol skills are beyond compare. After all, the reconnaissance man spends his days and nights way out in front of the other infantry troops conducting surveillance operations. One reason they do this is to designate targets for laser-guided bombs,

Marines and members of the Iraqi Security Forces watch as smoke pours from an abandoned vehicle in Karabilah during Operation Spear, conducted to destroy insurgency leadership strong points.

as well as ground and naval artillery. Finally, Force Recon Marines are trained to rescue hostages and prisoners of war.

The Force Recon concept was brought to life at Camp Pendleton, the Marine Corps base in California. It began with an experimental recon team that was later merged with an amphibious reconnaissance company to form the 1st Force Reconnaissance Company. Over the years, Force Reconnaissance has existed in many different forms. It has been expanded and contracted, but it has always remained a force ready to land with an MEU (SOC) anywhere in the world within six hours of an order.

Structurally, a Force Recon company looks much like an infantry battalion, as opposed to a standard company. Generally, it is commanded by a lieutenant colonel, with a major as the executive officer. The subsequent list of standard personnel includes a sergeant major and administrative, intel-

ligence, operations, logistics, and communications officers. One of the platoons within the company is a scout/sniper platoon on loan from the MEU's battalion landing team.

Interestingly, much of the equipment used by Force Recon Marines is standard issue within the other branches. However, they do have some equipment that is uniquely suited for their purposes, such as specially designed armored vests, integrated communications helmets, modified pistols, and a jeep-like fast attack vehicle. But with few exceptions, the success of Force Recon missions is in the hands of specially trained Marines using the same weapons as any other U.S. soldiers.

The missions of Force Recon generally fall into two categories: greenside operations and direct action operations. Greenside operations are those that aren't likely to involve direct contact with opposing forces. Most of the traditional Force Recon missions fall into this area. For example, they include

Staff Sergeant Raymond T. Bradway, platoon sergeant of Command Security Detachment 2, Regimental Combat Team 8, 2nd Marine Division, provides security during elections held in Fallujah, Iraq, on December 15, 2005. *Lance Corporal Josh Cox*

U.S. forces secure a street in Iraq after an improvised explosive device detonated in Baghdad. Marine Corps Systems Command uses computer analysis of past events to attempt to forecast future IED activity. *Air Force Staff Sergeant Reynaldo Ramon*

deep recon patrols that are so far behind enemy lines that they can't receive artillery support or helicopter extractions. Rather than using defensive weapons, a deep recon patrol team relies more on techniques of stealth and evasion to reach their objective. In fact, body armor is rarely employed during greenside operations because of its bulk and the noise it makes in motion.

Direct action operations, also called blackside operations, are those that will almost definitely involve direct contact with unwelcoming enemies. Examples of such missions include tactical recovery of aircraft personnel (TRAP), gas/oil platform (GOPLAT) raids, vessel board/search/seizures (VBSS), and others. If necessary for the mission at hand, direct action units will pick up special operators for very specific tasks such as ordnance disposal or electronic warfare. These units don't waste any time with a stealthy approach. They swoop into the area of their objective in their fast-attack vehicles, by helicopter, by parachute, or by sea. And they'll leave just as quickly,

only when they do, there will most likely be a stunned enemy left to try to explain to his superiors what just happened.

Snipers

The term "sniper" originated in India and was a reference to the snipe, a bird that was so difficult to shoot that only the most disciplined and talented hunters could hit it. The M40 weapons system was introduced during Vietnam, as was the two-man sniper team. Analysis after the fact brought to light an interesting discovery. Infantry Marines, with their fully automatic weapons, were laying down heavy blankets of fire that resulted in one kill for every 15,000 rounds fired. Snipers, on the other hand, scored one kill every 1.2 rounds fired. It didn't take long for the Corps to realize the value of a specialized sniper weapon and all the training necessary to master it. The M40A3 sniper rifle was developed in Quantico and, with few modifications, is still the sharpshooter's weapon of choice.

It's important to remember that regardless of a Marine's role within the Corps, one thing remains constant: each Marine is a rifleman. There are many advantages to this phi-

Marines from Company L, 3rd Battalion, 6th Marine Regiment, provide security while members of their platoon search and clear a building in Husayba, Iraq, during Operation Steel Curtain on November 5, 2005. *Corporal Micah Snead*

losophy that has become a proud tradition for the Marine Corps. For one, military forces around the world employ fire teams in battle. Only the Marines have cooks and supply clerks who can lead those teams . Another benefit to having a basically trained force capable of shooting accurately from as far away as five hundred yards is the pool of Marines able to qualify as snipers. And some of them do go on to become the absolute best shooters in the world with one-shot, one-kill capabilities from one thousand yards or more. The skill of a Marine scout sniper is just one of the examples of the Marine ethos. Technology has nothing to do with it. It's all about the character of a Marine and his or her rifle.

Clearly, the firepower of the Marine Corps is significant, and with such specialized training, it's all in capable hands.

Opposite page: Sergeant Memo M. Sandoval, a platoon sergeant with Scout Sniper Platoon, Headquarters and Service Company, 3rd Battalion, 5th Marine Regiment, stopped Iraqi insurgents from launching further mortar attacks against his fellow Marines. The sergeant made the shots from a distance of 950 yards.

But to an enemy, the psychological impact of being overwhelmed by a single Marine can be more frightening than the prospect of coming face to face with American ordnance. Nothing imparts that fear more than the prospect of being in the crosshairs of a Marine scout sniper. Capable of lying in wait for days at a time in any weather, these Marines do more than just sprawl flat on the ground: they become the ground. And they see the world through nothing but their rifle scope, all in anticipation of a single shot.

In his book, *Jarhead*, Anthony Swofford discusses his experiences in the first Gulf War as a Marine scout sniper. He talks about the stories American forces heard during the buildup to that war, which described how fierce the Iraqi army would be. Those stories were based on how ferociously these men had fought throughout the 1980s during the Afghan civil war. Apparently, the Iraqis had been told the same thing about the American military and the Marines in particular, because they put up very little fight. Rather than having to endure surprise attacks and fearless, charging mili-

Marines with 2nd Squad, 2nd Platoon, Company B, 1st Battalion, 6th Marine Regiment, patrol toward a ruined structure bordering Tharthar Lake's shoreline. Company B personnel participated in Operation Dagger, a five-day-long effort to rid regions north of Fallujah of insurgent activity.

tants, the Marines were forced to figure out what to do with thousands of voluntarily surrendering soldiers. It's not that some of the Iraqis didn't put up a fight; it's just that there weren't enough of them left to mount a united attack.

Snipers have been used by the Marines since they were first deployed on navy ships in the 1700s as a ship-board police crew. At that time, they were positioned in the bird's nest atop the ship's mast. They are now part of two-man advance scout teams that can crawl to a surprisingly close proximity to enemy objectives for surveillance purposes. While one member of the team relentlessly scans for targets of opportunity, the other waits with his sniper rifle at the ready.

Artillery

While the tradition of every Marine being a rifleman is not likely to end anytime soon, there will always be a role for the power, range, and effect that artillery brings to the battle. For the Corps, artillery is not meant to replace infantry units; rather, they coexist in a unique way. Marines, no matter their role, train for one thing and one thing only: to win battles. That's what enables armored tank and infantry battalions to train their companies separately yet still have them prepared to split off and seamlessly team up for combat operations.

Advance warning isn't usually an option on the battlefield. All it takes is a Marine to overlook one sliver of a degree on patrol and an enemy will seize the opportunity. If it had happened in Iraq in 2005, the desert would have erupted into a shower of sand and chaos in a split second. A series of mortar rounds would have fallen. Marines would have scrambled for cover. With no idea of the direction from which the projectiles came, there would have been nothing else they could have done until the strike ended.

The enemies of the Marine Corps, for the most part, rarely have sufficient technology to help their forward observers correct for errors during a strike. They soon find

Lance Corporal Steven L. Phillips stands at Camp Al Qa'im, Iraq, with his shotgun and Mk 152 shoulder-mounted antitank weapon, ready to advance if called. Behind him in support is Lance Corporal Paul J. Kolkhorst. Both Marines are antitank assaultmen and participated in Operation Steel Curtain with Company I, 3rd Battalion, 6th Marine Regiment, Regimental Combat Team 2. *Sergeant Jerad W. Alexander*

out that, unless they were spot on target the first time, all they've done is announce their own position to the Marines, who have better guns and better technology.

While the Marines do have a few men who carry the title of forward observer, they train all their riflemen in the basic techniques necessary to call in fire. They could be patrol leaders or LAV commanders. In recon platoons, the scout snipers are often the ones who do it. Even to an observer scanning the horizons with high-powered target-acquisition scopes, an underground bunker in the desert looks a whole lot like all the other sand dunes around it. But when you're a recon Marine, it doesn't take much to notice that something about one sand dune is different from all the rest. Call it instinct. Call it training. Whatever it is, the sniper's about to call down the destruction.

His options are numerous. He can call in planes, helicopters, or heavy artillery. Just as a sniper lives for one-shot, one-kill success, an artillery unit's goal is to score a decisive,

direct hit the first time. Anything else will only announce their intention to the enemy and give them time to take cover. So, the forward observer carefully relays coordinates to the fire direction center (FDC).

Generally, the FDC is located far away from the guns themselves, for obvious reasons. However, since artillery units are always on the move, there's really no point in setting up a central location. Once an observer calls in a mission to the FDC, the battery is alerted with a warning order that sends the crew racing into position. As the firing data is received, the crew confirms the information by repeating it. Trajectory, amount of powder (charge), and traverse angle are all part of the order. Once the orders are sent and confirmed, the FDC issues the "Fire!" command, then calls the observer and informs him of the shot. The observer watches the round fall and then offers corrections. Of course, the prevalence of global positioning systems (GPS) throughout

A UH-1 Huey helicopter takes off on a routine mission over the Al Qa'im region of Iraq. One of the helicopters' crew chiefs flexes his muscles as a show of confidence to the Marines on the ground. Hueys are used for a variety of mission in the Al Qa'im region. *Corporal James D. Hamel*

all facets of the battlefield generally makes the corrections minimal, if at all necessary.

When artillery is necessary, odds are good that the M198 155mm howitzer will be the gun of choice. Deadly accurate with its six-inch rounds to a distance of fifteen miles, or almost nineteen miles with rocket-assisted ordnance, the M198 can fire a maximum of four rounds per minute. More realistically, it will fire two rounds per minute, but that's a pace that the gun can keep up for as long as its nine-man crew is able.

The real skill of the howitzer's crew, though, is the time-on-target (TOT) mission. Firing a mortar is relatively simple, but like hitting a golf ball, getting it to go where you want it to when it's supposed to be there requires skill. Putting three rounds in the same place at the same time also takes skill, as well as a fair amount of math. The same crew fires three rounds in succession that land simultaneously on the same target. The first round follows a high arch, the second follows a somewhat lower path, and the third takes a flat trajectory. Done properly, the snipers who called in the coordinates will not see a quick succession of boom, boom, boom. Rather, the target will become a crater with one thunderous roar, and afterward all that's left is silence.

As if the M198 wasn't powerful enough, it is about to be replaced by the M777 ultralightweight howitzer. They both have the same 155mm bore and two-rounds-per-minute sustained rate of fire. The main differences are that the M777 weighs almost 42 percent less than its predecessor thanks to its titanium construction, requires two fewer crewmembers, and most impressively, has almost twice as much range. The expanded reach of the new howitzer helps

Various weapons systems and equipment were seized following the fighting between insurgents and Marines with 2nd Battalion, 4th Marine Regiment, and soldiers from 1st Brigade Combat Team (BCT). The firefight began shortly after a convoy carrying the commander of 1st BCT was attacked with an improvised explosive device. Marines with Mobile Assault Company and Company G, 2nd Battalion, 4th Marine Regiment, reinforced 1st BCT and killed twenty-one enemy fighters.

keep more Marines out of the direct line of fire. Plus, its lighter weight increases the mobility of the force and thus its effectiveness. And that's not easy to do since crews already train to get into firing position, set up the gun, receive their fire mission, shoot, and get back on the road before the rounds even hit the target.

Like most things they do, the Marine Corps uses armor differently than other military forces. Not that the Marines don't have armor, but the AAVs and LAVs they rely on are considerably lighter than the M1A1 Abrams tanks they operate in fewer numbers. So the army lines up its tanks and goes after an enemy force head to head, and the Marines use their tanks as security for their lighter armored vehicles that are sus-

ceptible to anything over .50-caliber, particularly the missiles specifically designed to penetrate them. And when it's time to break through enemy lines, the M1A1 is just right for the job.

The infantry will always serve an important role. But the ability of an artillery unit to lay down heavy fire and then pile it on in conjunction with the rest of the task force can do more than turn tables when necessary. It can win wars.

Close-Air Support

Because an infantry Marine's mission is to take his place at the tip of the spear, the Corps' air fleet consists of fixed and rotor-wing aircraft that serve as the spear's gleaming and lethal point. Not long after the thump-thump-thump of a

A four-ton pile of captured enemy ammunition has been prepped to be destroyed in a massive explosion at a site in Iraq's Al Anbar Province. At one point, the site housed the largest stash of munitions found in western Iraq. Workers cleared the site of approximately twelve thousand tons of bombs, mortars, grenades, and bullets, which insurgents could have used to attack troops and Iraqis. A U.S. Army battalion worked with the 1st Force Service Support Group to rid Al Anbar Province of weapons found throughout Saddam Hussein's former regime.

CH-46E Sea Knight or a CH-53E helicopter is heard, it comes into view with its primary cargo of battle-ready Marines. Enemy soldiers know all too well that close behind are a few AH-1W Cobra attack helicopters. Iraqi soldiers call them the "skinny birds" for good reason. Designed with a narrow profile to provide as small a target to the enemy as possible, the pilot actually sits above and behind the gunner. The Cobra is an agile aircraft that provides cover fire for Marines departing a transport. With an armament of Hellfire anti-tank missiles, Sidewinder air-to-air missiles, and Sidearm antiradiation missiles, the Marines inside are well equipped to defend themselves or the troops on the ground.

Close-air support (CAS) is a mission that is unique to Marine aviation, but like everything else, it's closely linked to the ultimate mission of the Corps. Here's how it works:

Marines on the ground will fan out in fire teams and call in coordinates for enemy locations. Not long afterward, the jets fly over and the fireworks start. It all happens very quickly.

The same ships that launched many of these Marines in an amtrac only a day or so earlier also house the AV-8B Harrier II jets that are unique to the Corps. Small enough to fit on shipboard elevators, the Harrier II can perform a vertical takeoff and landing (VTOL). However, training accidents and fuel studies have proven the short takeoff, vertical landing (STOVL) to be more efficient. Rather than lifting straight off the deck of the ship and running the risk of encountering problems during the transition from vertical to horizontal flight, the pilot executes a short takeoff roll, making the transition much safer.

Newer models have incorporated the same radar system as the F/A-18 Hornet, giving the Harrier the ability to carry

Private Jefferson J. Haney, a 25-year-old native of Fresno, California, patrols the streets that surround Camp Blue Diamond in Ar Ramadi, Iraq. Jefferson was an artilleryman with Battery L, 3rd Battalion, 10th Marine Regiment, before his entire battery was converted into a provisional rifle company to provide security for the 2nd Marine Division's headquarters element. *Sergeant Ryan S. Scranton*

AIM-120 AMRAAM missiles, whereas older models used in the first Gulf War were limited to day flight. However, limitations in the Corps only provide Marines with opportunities to prove their skills. To avoid Iraqi fire, the Harriers stayed well above ten thousand feet, so the typical attack involved a forty-five-degree dive on a target that wasn't easy to spot in the first place. The unguided bombs would be dropped between ten thousand and seven thousand feet. The results were unquestionable. Lieutenant Colonel Dick White had this to say about the Harrier's effectiveness during the first Gulf War:

"We launched four aircraft. They made two passes each, releasing the one-thousand-pound bombs right onto the artillery pieces themselves. We watched the video of the sortie, and you could actually see the big 122mm guns going end over end as though they were toys."

— Lieutenant Colonel Dick White, USMC, VMA-311

And to think, the Corps has remanufactured the entire fleet of Harriers to be even more effective.

The preceding section is not meant to be a review of the capabilities of all the equipment used by Marines at war. However, it is meant to provide a foundation for a discussion of how Marines fought wars in the early twenty-first century. And it provides a basic understanding of the Marines' core strengths so that we can look more closely at the style of warfare they employ.

Styles of Warfare

The chaotic nature of war prevents it from being characterized precisely. Instead, the various ways a war can be fought exist on a spectrum. At one end is warfare by attrition, or the complete destruction of enemy personnel and equipment. At the other is warfare by maneuver, which attacks the enemy's system instead of the enemy's arsenal. Every battle of every war is fought somewhere between the two extremes.

Warfare by Attrition

Winning a war by attrition is a long and ugly process. Attrition within a corporate setting could mean departing clients or departing staff members. In warfare it means dying troops—lots of them, and quite frankly, this is simply not an acceptable method to the general public. Pure attrition warfare doesn't actually exist, since, in its most basic terms, it requires superior equipment, more personnel, and the ability to bomb and strike so thoroughly that there is nothing left of the enemy. There's not a military force in the world that won't surrender before it comes to that.

Attritional success requires the ability to inflict mass casualties while sustaining troop strength as the enemy is depleted through losses. A military force engaged in this type of fight must be constantly training and shipping new soldiers to the front to replace those lost to enemy fire. Not only does this run the risk of degrading public support for a war effort, but it also doesn't do much for troop morale.

It's not that Marines have never found themselves engaged in a fight that simply required them to handle a great loss of life and still overcome enemy forces. In fact, the mission of the Marine Corps makes this a possibility every time it is called to action. So, not surprisingly, the Marines have added to their legend in situations, such as the Chosin Reservoir, that should have spelled their sure demise, by fighting and surviving with far fewer men than the enemy.

Wars can't be fought without attrition. It's the hardest part for any leader to swallow when sending young men and women into battle zones. Whether it's the president or the young lieutenant on his first tour, all leaders bear a sense of responsibility for the lives of their troops. And it's that sense of accountability that has led the Marines to their own version of warfare by maneuver.

Warfare by Maneuver

When you can outmaneuver and out-plan your opponent, there is much less risk of losing lives. Warfare by maneuver is based on strategic strikes from a position of advantage against locations that are critical to an enemy's system. Whether it's attacking a weapons depot or a command facility, or both at the same time, the Marines will execute orders quickly and with decisive power. The strike may come from the air or from ground troops, or again, both at the same time. No matter the way in which a strike is delivered, it will come from over the horizon, and you can be sure that it will pit a Marine strength against an enemy weakness.

Another element of success from warfare by maneuver is surprise coupled with speed. Physics tells us that speed over time creates tempo. The success of the Corps tells us that tempo is a weapon that's just as effective as any rifle. Catching an enemy off guard creates disorder and confusion. The faster you pile on the attacks from all angles, the faster the situation degrades for the enemy. Unfortunately, the same principles can affect the Marines. The difference is that Marines seem to operate on a totally different plane than most of their enemies. And that's why they win, even when things don't start off looking very good for them.

Ramadi— Turning Ambush into Victory

On April 6, 2004, Echo Company, 2nd Battalion, 4th Marines (abbreviated as 2/4), was called to provide support for one of its sniper patrols that was under fire in Ramadi, Iraq. Shortly after heading out, however, they received a follow-on call saying that the snipers had pushed back with enough force to send the enemy on its way. But the 1st Platoon was experiencing heavy fire in the city and they needed help. Their commanding officer, Captain Kelly Royer, arranged for his men to meet up with Lieutenant John "Ski" Wroblewski and his team at an intersection near the marketplace. What they didn't know was that Iraqi fighters had made their way through that same marketplace earlier in the day. Along the way, they instructed the shopkeepers to close up for the day because there was an ambush in the works, and they were planning to kill Americans.

The 2/4 had already suffered more casualties than any other battalion since the war had begun more than a year earlier. And Echo Company had borne the brunt of the loss, with twenty-three dead.

As Lieutenant "Ski" and his men approached in Humvees and trucks, Iraqi and foreign fighters unloaded with everything they had. AK-47s, machine guns, and ocket-propelled grenades seemed to be coming at both units om all directions. The surprise attack had been very well lanned and executed. Marines were taking fire from rooftops f the low-lying buildings, from behind trees, and from with- 1 the purposely empty market stalls.

The first Humvee slowed as it rolled into the marketplace. he Marines inside ranged from eighteen-year-old PFCs (pri- ate first class) and lance corporals to veteran staff sergeants nd a navy corpsman. In total, there were eight Marines. Only ne would survive the battle. The others barely survived the irst few minutes. From the other Humvees close behind, seven iflemen poured out and headed for cover.

If there can be comedic relief in a situation like this, it ame in the form of the Iraqi translator, dubbed "007" by the Marines. Like everyone else, he was running for cover, but he vas the only one smiling as he did so. He was wearing a sleeve- ess sweat suit, tan sandals, and a navy blue T-shirt that said Operation Iraqi Freedom." With no helmet and no vest, he imply believed he would survive if he were meant to.

Captain Royer led his Marines to the roof of the house n which they had taken cover. The house was under heavy ire, and the roof provided a better vantage point from which o survey the battle and call in fire support from air assets. Jnfortunately, none of the helicopters could break away from he firefights they were supporting at other points around own. Lieutenant Wroblewski was evacuated under emer- ency medical care after a bullet pierced the radio handset he vas holding and hit his face. He died later when medics were inable to stop the bleeding.

Back on the rooftop, Captain Royer dispatched a fire eam to take out the machine gun, but the gunners had lready left their position. One by one, the Marines secured ooftops in the vicinity, which enabled them to take control of he marketplace intersection. Gradually, the gunfire faded out, but not before ten Echo Company Marines had been ost. That day, the Marines of 2/4 were forced to fight a battle of attrition. However, their determination and pride were too great to allow the first few minutes of the ambush to dictate he end result. Once they were able to gain an understanding of the situation, they employed the methods they had been aught and took control.

Marines located Fedayeen bunkers full of weapons and ammunition outside Jaman Al Juburi.

Only a few days later, still recovering from the devasta- tion earlier in the week, Echo Company picked up a mission to secure an area by going house to house on foot. They were up and out before sunrise, with illumination flares lighting the scene. The Marines were making progress, interrogating and detaining each of the local men. Erratic bursts of gunfire began to ring out all around them. Then it picked up. Captain Royer took a shot in the head that proved to be an uninten- tional display of the power of a Kevlar helmet. The high- powered round hit his helmet, knocking it off, but didn't even come close to breaking through. He simply put it back on and resumed the fight.

Working hard to reach cover, Echo Company was still taking gunfire from everywhere. Finally, the helicopters responded. The sound of the rotors slicing the air must have been music to their ears. With three devastating passes of machine-gun fire, the fight ended just as quickly as it began.

Operation Enduring Freedom

Speed is a critical factor in gaining an advantage and turning it into momentum. Whichever side is gaining momentum gets to call the shots. The enemy has no choice but to backpedal in reaction to the chaos and simply try to keep up. Operation Enduring Freedom provided an example of the scalability of the Marine Corps and its ability to operate successfully under the doctrine of maneuver warfare. The relatively small size of the Corps and its expeditionary training makes it extremely agile. This gives it the ability to execute orders with speed and precision. It's also what enables the Corps to capitalize on success as it happens and see firsthand the result of continued strikes. Couple that with the trust that Marine commanders place in their enlisted troops to call in fire on opportune targets, and you have the recipe for a downward spiral of events that the enemy never sees coming.

On October 7, 2001, a squadron of F/A-18 Hornets, along with bombers from other branches, streaked across a stretch of Middle Eastern desert. The immediate objectives were to carry out the destruction of terrorist training camps and the infrastructure within Afghanistan, while also delivering humanitarian aid to the citizens. The operation was named Operation Enduring Freedom and was the first strike in the U.S.-led war on terrorism. Enemy fighters in Afghanistan were unaware of the technology possessed by the Americans, so much so that U.S. spotters were often able to pinpoint locations for the aircraft overhead by the enemy soldiers standing out in the open on top of their position.

The ultimate goal was to capture the leaders of the al Qaeda terrorist organization in order to disrupt or, better yet, stop any further operations. Because the majority of al Qaeda's training bases were allowed in Afghanistan by the Taliban regime, its leaders and operations became a primary target as well. Within two weeks, virtually all Taliban air defenses were completely destroyed. It was evident, however, that just the air strikes would not be enough. In order to totally root out enemy fighters and break down the Taliban for good, ground forces would be necessary.

Planning for the ground operation was a long process that started well before any action was initiated. Brigadier General James N. Mattis confirmed that the operation would be more of a marathon than a sprint. In other words, it wouldn't be the quick-strike mission that the Marines are known for. They would be on the ground for some time conducting many different missions. In fact, by the time they had packed up and washed down, the Marines of 15th MEU (SOC) and 26th MEU (SOC) had planned or conducted nineteen of twenty-three tasks from the MAGTF's mission essential task list. Together, the two MEU (SOC)s formed Task Force 58, and their efforts helped ensure the Taliban's collapse.

On November 25, 2001, Charlie Company, Battalion Landing Team (BLT) 1/1's heliborne forces departed USS Peleliu. Two waves of CH-53Es were escorted ashore by AH-1W Cobras and UH-1 Hueys, and the combined force were able to secure a dirt airstrip without any resistance. The next night, just after sundown, two Cobras engaged three armored vehicles near a Taliban stronghold in what would be the first of many skirmishes in the area of Forward Operating Base (FOB) Rhino. Two of the three vehicles and numerous Taliban soldiers were destroyed with assistance from two navy aircraft.

Conditions at Rhino were miserable at best. The sand had the consistency of talcum powder, and the slightest disturbance would kick up a cloud that hung in the air for fifteen minutes or more. It's easy to imagine the constant dust that remained airborne after a night of helicopters taking off and landing from the air field. And when there's constant dust, Marines constantly clean their weapons. Not that they mind; to a Marine, cleaning his weapon is like a basketball player retying his shoes three or four times during a game. It just feels right. In addition to the dust, there was the daily swing in temperatures. During the day it would soar to above eighty degrees, while at night the temperature would plummet to thirty or lower. Every morning, the Marines would wake up with frost on their parkas and ice in their canteens.

Several days later, on December 6, security forces at Rhino spotted flashes in the sky to the north of the FOB. Naval P-3 patrol aircraft circling far overhead confirmed that vehicles were being loaded, and BLT 1/1 engaged them with 81mm mortars. After the assault, an LAV patrol was sent out

Marines from 1st Platoon, Charley Company, 1st Battalion, 7th Marine Regiment, Regimental Combat Team (RCT) 7, provide security, scanning the thick vegetation of Haqlaniyah Island for movement as other Marines clear the first objective during the island assault.

to investigate the site, but found no personnel or equipment. Remaining flights for that evening were cancelled, but the night was just getting started, as it turned out.

Later that night, Marines along Route 1 engaged in a firefight. P-3s overhead reported six vehicles headed toward their roadblock. The vehicles came to a stop, and then one vehicle sped toward the wire obstacle crossing the road. It stopped when it got tangled in the wire, and the Marines pounded it with gunfire, setting it aflame. One person in the truck attempted to run even though he was on fire. He was stopped short by a Marine sniper. The ensuing explosion of the truck sent the remaining enemies scattering to the north of the road. The P-3 observer spotted no more than 30 of them. The observer, along with a Marine forward air controller (FAC), directed fire for CAS aircraft, and each vehicle and many of the

enemy soldiers were destroyed. Estimates place the number of enemy dead at around 120. Not surprisingly, no movement was reported along the route for several days.

In mid-December, the 15th MEU (SOC)'s LAR Company moved through the city of Kandahar and secured the airport for follow-on forces. Before sunup, helicopters from both the 15th and 26th MEU (SOC) were flying reinforcements into the air field. With the airport secure, the 26th MEU was then able to move down into southern Afghanistan. As with most of the other operations completed in Afghanistan in 2001, there was very little incident involved with taking the Kandahar airport. The extent of American casualties was three Marines wounded in a land mine explosion. All three survived and were awarded Purple Hearts.

By mid-December, Kabul was firmly in the hands of anti-Taliban forces. Ultimately, within a few more short months, the Taliban was completely removed from power and the al Qaeda network within Afghanistan was crushed.

You might think removing a totalitarian government and rendering it virtually irrelevant in a matter of months would require absolute destruction. But combining force, speed, and precision during those first couple of weeks in October 2001 seized the initiative, which enabled American and coalition forces to act at will throughout the process as they focused exclusively on their targets.

The 15th MEU (SOC)'s role in Operation Enduring Freedom came to an end on January 18, 2002. They had conducted operations ranging from humanitarian assistance to combat actions by both ground and air. Some Marines had

pent 139 consecutive days at sea, maintaining aircraft or flying missions over Afghanistan. Others had endured long months ashore under harsh conditions, providing security at the various air fields that were instrumental in beating back the Taliban and al Qaeda forces.

The proverbial "tyranny of distance" had been defeated, along with numerous equipment challenges. The actions of the 15th and 26th MEU (SOC)s provided indisputable evidence of the flexibility and capability of the MAGTF structure. Not only did the 15th MEU (SOC) prove its effectiveness over a greater distance than normal, it accomplished the deepest penetration of foreign territory ever by a force launched from the sea.

Being a Marine means that you are expected to step up to a leadership role when the situation calls for it. Whether in training, so that you'll be prepared to do it again, or in the midst of a fight, a Marine's goal is to never let his fellow Marines down. Honor, courage, and commitment are more than character traits; they are the reasons why yes men are few and far between in the Corps. They simply aren't tolerated. Now, there will always be instances in which a young Marine may get a little overzealous, but a commanding officer will use those situations as teaching opportunities, and young leaders know that. They don't use that fact as an excuse to run wild, but rather to act without fear of reprimand, knowing that they have the trust of senior officers. Ask any Marine if there's anything within the rules of engagement he can do in battle that will guarantee a harsh reprimand or worse, and the answer is unanimous: nothing. There is no place in war for a timid Marine.

A Marine with 1st Platoon, Company E, 2nd Battalion, 1st Marine Regiment, 1st Marine Division, watches over a captured terrorist who used tools to make improvised explosive devices in Fallujah, Iraq. The company entered Fallujah to begin the effort of removing insurgents from the city.

Chapter 3

THE CHANGING FACE OF WAR
FROM BATTLEFIELDS TO VILLAGES

There's no doubt that the nature of battle has changed drastically over the last few years. No longer does it play out on large, open battlefields. These days, wars are fought in urban areas. The Marines call it military operations on urban terrain (MOUT). No matter what you call it, it requires totally different training than traditional warfare. It's complicated by the fact that civilians are often close by. Then again, those who appear to be noncombatant citizens may actually be members of an armed militia. Or maybe they just don't like the idea of someone poking around their house and will defend it at any cost.

Limited fields of view and fire also cloud the water, as do the sheer number of places to hide. All those places that provide cover also offer opportunities for booby traps and snipers. Large military forces such as those of the United States would prefer that the fight stay out in the open. Traditional battlefields have been the source of many advances in battle technology. Heavy guns

and the ability to fire them with pinpoint accuracy have established the dominance of our military force around the world, which is exactly why weaker enemies will do everything they can to bring the fight into the closer confines of a city. It's much more difficult to conquer a town than an open field, due to the fact that it has to be done one building at a time. Those same buildings make it much easier for a smaller, less dominant force to defend its city. But perhaps the most significant factor is that international law prohibits the use of heavy artillery, tank assaults, and indiscriminate bombings from warplanes within civilian areas.

Guerrilla and insurgent tactics are so far outside the norm that larger forces are consistently taken by surprise. It seems as though it doesn't take long after the Marines or any other force catch on to one unorthodox method that another comes into play. One big challenge for American forces in the early twenty-first century is simply trying to figure out who it is that they're fighting.

Sergeant Phil F. "Mick" McCotter, a sniper with 2nd Battalion, 2nd Marine Regiment, scans the surrounding fields during a mission. The Marine and his team of snipers kept watch over the area as combat engineers scanned for weapons caches. The snipers were on the lookout for terrorists planting explosives or those trying to attack the Marines as they worked.

Opposite: Marines with Company K, 3rd Battalion, 25th Marine Regiment, and soldiers with Iraq Intervention Force, a branch of the Iraqi Army specifically trained in counterinsurgency operations, patrol the streets in Hit, Al Anbar.

Marines secure the perimeter around a house before they check it for weapons and insurgents.

In fact, debates are ongoing in many political circles about whether the type of war the coalition forces are involved in is a guerrilla war or if it is representative of true insurgents. Part of the debate stems from the fact that the term "insurgency" assumes that the current Iraqi government is established, although by all accounts it is shaky at best. As of now, the term is widely accepted, not just because it recognizes violence directed at the fledgling government of Iraq, but at coalition forces as well.

In June 2005, polls conducted within Iraq showed more and more antioccupation sentiment. The worst implication of this discovery was the rising support for the insurgency and the attacks they completed. Equally as damaging to the efforts of Marines and other coalition forces was the fact that this support made accurate intelligence harder and harder to come by. This fact was not lost on the insurgents themselves, who likely fed false information to the coalition in attempts to lure them into ambushes.

Insurgent groups conduct violent attacks involving quick-strike hit-and-run tactics that make them difficult to track down, much less return fire toward. Later, many of

Infantrymen from 1st Platoon, Company E, 2nd Battalion, 1st Marine Regiment, 1st Marine Division, look on from a rooftop as M1A1 tanks from 1st Tank Battalion fire on buildings where enemy snipers took positions. The company entered Fallujah to destroy enemy fighters who were attacking coalition forces from the city.

them will take to the airwaves or the Internet to claim the credit for having carried out an attack, just like terrorists. But also like terrorists, these groups rarely divulge the identity of their leaders. The addition of insurgents from countries outside of Iraq at times made the fight even more confusing. And while it may seem like a minor point, none of these groups wore uniforms, making it very difficult to determine which group someone was fighting for, and it also forced Marines to decide whether someone actually posed a danger to them.

Civilian casualties and massive amounts of property damage are practically unavoidable no matter how a battle

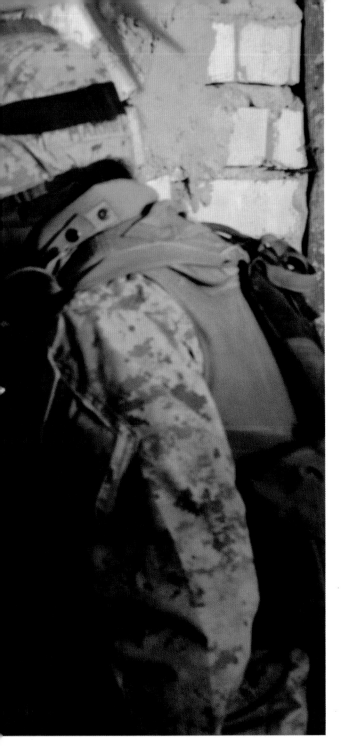

The cost to the attacking force can be extreme when dealing with insurgents in an urban setting, not only in the extra resources required to spread out within an urban area, but more importantly from the loss of troops. Being unfamiliar with the layout of the city puts them at a great disadvantage. This was evident in the aftermath of the October 3, 1993, Battle of Mogadishu in which eighteen American soldiers were killed and another seventy-nine wounded. It also inspired the USMC Warfighting Laboratory to create a whole program entitled Operation Urban Warrior.

Operation Urban Warrior

Dubbed the most important program in the military due to the increase of urban fields of battle, Operation Urban Warrior has proven that the infantry rifleman is far from obsolete. Modern weapons and technology work wonders out in the open, but city streets are no place for an M1A1 Abrams tank. Clearly, there's still no replacement for a Marine and his rifle.

The primary mission of the urban warrior is to fight enemies in urban environments. Without sounding too simplistic, it's important to mention that, because accomplishing that mission involves more than shooting a rifle. Not everyone in an urban area is an enemy. Figuring out who's who often requires a good relationship with the people themselves. So the urban warrior also engages in quite a few humanitarian efforts in order to gain the trust of the people.

Often, these urban warriors must do both within a matter of minutes. This presents an interesting challenge to Marines, and it definitely tests their discipline. It would be very easy to take out the frustration of being shot at from some hidden location on the next person who opens a door. But doing so would go against everything Marines are taught. While the answer to most problems usually means developing a new technology, the Marines are seeing results from just adding to the already impressive training of their infantrymen.

Gulf War II

The start of the second Gulf War was supposed to illustrate another key to the Marines' success: surprise. While even rudimentary technology and radar systems prevent any enemy from being oblivious to an oncoming attack, the objective is to

plays out. And the smaller force will use those losses to add fuel to the fire. When the world sees photos and video of dead civilians and crumbling buildings, sympathy is often expressed for their plight, and the morale of the larger force can begin to wither away.

Further complicating matters in Iraq were counterinsurgency efforts. Many counterinsurgency operations end up killing more civilians than the insurgents. Tactics range from ordinary policing to actions just shy of conventional warfare.

be so close to the target that it's too late to mount any serious defense by the time the enemy is aware of the danger.

While it may be impossible to maintain a high rate of speed of maneuver over an extended period of time, there is no doubt that it has its advantages. The ability it gives the Marines to concentrate superior strength at a decisive time and place is clear. It also does wonders for the security of Marines, because they're the ones dictating the course of events, and thus they have the luxury of knowing what's coming next.

Despite expectations, the beginning of the war turned out to be less than climactic: that is, until the details became available. Credible intelligence had disclosed the location of Saddam Hussein, and the jets were sent in to take advantage. Special forces were already on the ground. So rather than simultaneous attacks on air defenses, palaces, ammunition stores, and other locations critical to the Iraqi system, we saw a scaled-down version directed exclusively at Saddam Hussein. Not that attacks against the Iraqi system didn't come later, but one of the cardinal rules of maneuver warfare is to take advantage of any opportunity that presents itself.

When those attacks did come against key Iraqi locations, they were well planned. In the course of that planning, many questions were asked: What can the enemy not do without? And of those, which can we exploit the most rapidly for maximum impact?

So it's not surprising that the first target would be one of Saddam's many palaces. Nor was it surprising that many of the subsequent targets would be his other palaces. But not all of these critical targets are physical structures. Many of them are vague, like enemy morale, and that is exactly why Marines immediately moved into the bombed-out palaces once occupied by the men who brought so much fear to the people of Iraq. To see their own enemies practically vacationing in these estates left no doubt that the government they were fighting to defend was not only bent, but also badly broken.

Boldness in battle is a trait for which the Marines are famous. In fact, it's written into their *Warfighting* doctrine. Because war is full of uncertainty, Marines are trained to make the most of any advantage they uncover. It's how they turn a series of minor victories into major results. This is not a new philosophy. Napoleon Bonaparte once said, "The

battlefield is a scene of chaos. The winner will be the one who controls that chaos, both his own and the enemy's."

Nasiriyah

If the ground campaign was to make any progress, it would have to do so by going through Nasiriyah. Knowing that Nasiriyah was a stronghold for Iraqi soldiers and that those soldiers knew the Marines were headed in that direction, the staff devised a plan to surprise them by going around the town and closing them in to the north and south.

At least that's the way it was supposed to happen when the 1st Battalion, 2nd Marines sent its three infantry compa-

Marines with Company B, 1st Battalion, 6th Marine Regiment, sweep through a ruined building, searching for weapons and explosive devices as part of Operation Dagger in the Thar region north of Fallujah, Iraq.

nies into Nasiriyah on March 23, 2003. The mission was to secure the bridges at the north and south ends of the city to clear the way for more units to continue north to Baghdad. Alpha Company was to lead the way in from the south and secure the southern bridge. Bravo Company would come in behind them and sweep to the east of the city because the direct road between the two bridges had become known as "Ambush Alley" due to the number of buildings that could be used as hiding places along both sides of the road. Once

outside the eastern city limits, Bravo Company was to set up a support position for Charlie Company to follow in behind them and push on to the northern bridge. All in all, it was a tactically sound and well-thought-out plan that would have worked perfectly had it been just a training exercise.

The fog of war, however, has a way of changing plans. The element of surprise was blown when a misdirected army supply convoy accidentally rolled up the road straight into town. The majority of the Marine Corps'

Two Marines with 2nd Squad, 3rd Platoon, Company C, 1st Battalion, 6th Marine Regiment, rush up a flight of stairs inside a building during Operation Hard Knock as they search through a home. Company C personnel worked alongside other battalion infantrymen and Iraqi Security Forces to search through a wired-off sector of Fallujah for weapons and insurgent activity, as well as to gather census information on the populace.

armor consists of light armored vehicles (LAV) and amphibious assault vehicles (AAV), neither of which have sides any thicker than a couple inches of aluminum and steel. That's why Marine M1A1 Abrams tanks were set to lead the way into Nasiriyah. Problem was, after an all-night run up to the city, the tanks were dangerously low on fuel. So when the time came for Alpha Company to start the charge, the tanks were still in the rear taking on fuel. Then things got really bad.

Fighting from every point of cover they could find, Marines began to realize that the Iraqis weren't scared to employ any tactic necessary. Mothers, fathers, and their kids would walk out of their houses in the midst of the gunfight, wave to the Marines in apparent gratitude, and then the father would produce an AK-47 from his robes and start firing. But

the real eye opener came when an ambulance drove full speed down the street with its siren going. When the ambulance refused to stop and was heading straight for a position held by a group of Marines, they had no choice but to fire into the cab of the truck. The ambulance veered to the side of the road and came to a stop. Immediately, five Iraqis poured out of the back with AK-47s. That's when it became clear that the two sides were following totally different rules of engagement.

As Bravo Company swung out to the east of Nasiriyah, its armored vehicles became bogged down in the mud. Essentially, they were sitting ducks, and the Marines inside quickly got out, making mad dashes in all directions. Communications were limited due to the effect of high-powered electrical lines close by. At that point, Charlie Company was coming over the south bridge and couldn't see he vehicles from Bravo anywhere. Their commanding officer ecided that Bravo must have taken the direct route through he city, so Charlie Company would do the same.

Making its way through the city, Charlie Company bsorbed machine-gun fire and was the target of several ocket-propelled grenade (RPG) attacks. One RPG hit an rmored vehicle at the northern end of the city, injuring a few Marines. But that was not the worst incident that these lentless Marines would face that day.

A pair of air force A-10s patrolling the area spotted what hey thought was an Iraqi mechanized unit north of the city. t was, in fact, Charlie Company. Having limped their way ut of the city after a couple of direct hits from RPGs, the hen of Charlie Company had unloaded from their armored vehicles and were setting up positions to hold the northern bridge. Since radio communications had been spotty at best, no one knew that the Marines of Charlie Company had even attempted to make it through Ambush Alley, much less that they had been successful. Their reward was a barrage of 30mm depleted uranium rounds from the nose guns of the A-10s. The Marines were sitting ducks. By the end, eighteen Marines were dead and twenty-four wounded.

Forced into retreat by friendly fire, Charlie Company made its way back into the city and took cover in a residential home that became known as "The Alamo." A three-hour gunfight ensued with the locals. All the while, one of the armored vehicle drivers was attempting to make contact with anyone who could help. By that time, the tanks had returned

Gunnery Sergeant Lee W. Sherwood, team leader, Explosive Ordnance Disposal, 8th Engineer Support Battalion, 2nd Force Service Support Group, sights in on a uspected improvised explosive device with a rifle. The team uses a specialized rifle to disarm or detonate these devices.

A Marine with 3rd Platoon, Company K, 3rd Battalion, 2nd Marine Regiment, Regimental Combat Team 2, engages a truck at the end of a road in Karabilah during Operation Spear.

from the rear and were in full force; an officer onboard one of the M1A1s picked up a faint signal from Charlie Company and was able to get a bead on their position. Only minutes later, the tanks arrived, and with a big show of force extracted the dead, wounded, and still-fighting Marines.

At the end of the day, the mission was accomplished. The north and south bridges into Nasiriyah were in the Marines' control. The price was larger than expected, but the nature of the Marines is to fight harder for the honor of their fallen brothers. Captain Ben Reid, an officer of Charlie Company, summed up the battle by stressing that it was the lance corporals and the PFCs who were making calls on the spot and decisions in

the interest of the mission that got them all through that battle. He noted that none of them would likely be rewarded for their actions that day, but Marines are used to that. They don't do it for the recognition, and when you understand that, you're just starting to understand the ethos of the Corps.

The fog of war was almost a blanket that day. But the *Warfighting* philosophy held true. When you anticipate chaos, you're never disappointed in battle. Even when you know what you're getting into, the disorder can be overwhelming. But when you're expecting one set of circumstances and find another, it can be downright crippling. Unless you're a Marine.

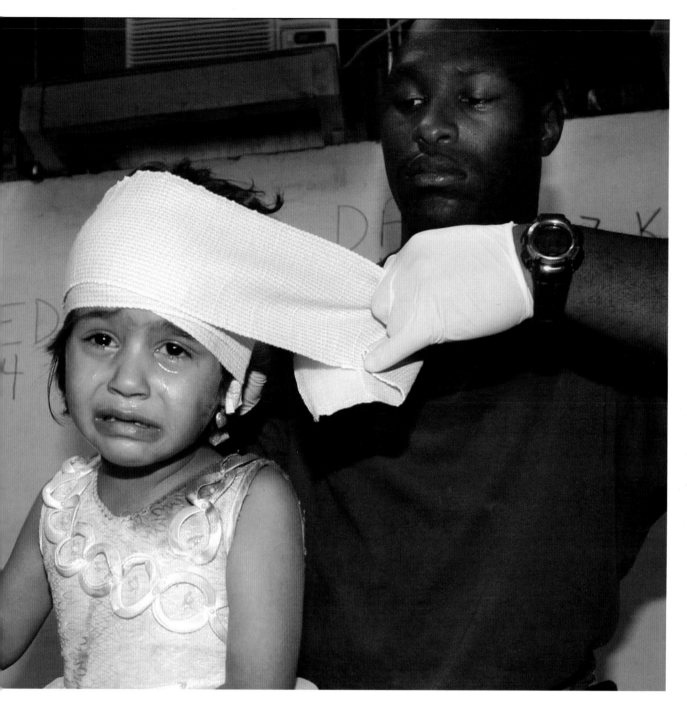

Corpsman Robert D. Bush loosens the bandage on an injured Iraqi girl's head at Camp Hadithah Dam. The 3rd Battalion, 25th Marine Regiment, aid station is equipped to handle everything from a routine sick call to combat trauma injuries. The corpsmen are on call twenty-four hours a day to treat the injured.

Umm Qasr

Only a few days before the battle at Nasiriyah, Marines of Echo Company, Second Battalion, First Marines of the 15th Marine Expeditionary Unit (Special Operations Capable) were met with circumstances that were completely different than what they expected. Echo Company had been designated the mechanized unit of 15th MEU's ground combat element. They had amtracs and four tanks, which established them as the main effort (the unit with primary responsibility for the mission) for all infantry missions. They had practiced assaults and raids of all scopes out in the desert at Twentynine Palms, California, and amphibious assaults in San Diego. They were ready, and yet they would be surprised on the first day of fighting.

Military police Marines from Marine Wing Support Squadron (MWSS) 374, Marine Wing Support Group 37, 3rd Marine Aircraft Wing, take cover as explosive ordnance disposal technicians, also from MWSS 374, detonate an improvised explosive device in Khaldiya, Iraq. The MWSS 374 Marines are from the Marine Corps Air Ground Combat Center, Twentynine Palms, California.

For several weeks prior to the assault, the Marines had been keeping an eye on the port town. Aerial photographs had shown little if any activity, much less any attempt at so much as a buildup. So a plan was created, rehearsed, and studied by all involved. As they were planning the attack on Umm Qasr at the start of the war, they were expecting only a miniscule force of about thirty-five enemy troops, fighting with little more than small arms.

At 5:00 a.m. on that morning in late March, Echo Company rolled out of its staging area in Kuwait for an hour's drive in the amtracs up to Umm Qasr. But around 5:30 a.m., they began to hear reports of a larger group of Iraqis ready to defend the town. Then, when they were fifteen minutes from the border, they received what must have been a chilling phone call. It seemed that there was, in fact, a brigade-size force waiting for them on the other side.

During the few days in which the Marines had ceased to pull aerial pictures of the town, Saddam had sent an infantry brigade south to defend the port. Within moments, what was supposed to have been little more than slight resistance turned into full conflict. The plans that had been developed were instantly irrelevant. This highlights one of the main thrusts of the *Warfighting* philosophy: never fall in love with your battle plans, because they'll only betray you if you do. Everyone must be able to support a strategy, but they must be just as willing to toss it out as soon as necessary.

What the Marines did instead was to prepare the best they could for a movement to contact. Smaller units were

Corporal Eric R. Hamilton, a fire team leader with Company I, 3rd Battalion, 25th Marine Regiment, provides security as his squad enters a building in Hit, Al Anbar.

spread out and acted with the commander's intent and some general guidance. When it was all said and done, the Marines had captured 426 Iraqi regulars and killed an unconfirmed number. And the Marines had accomplished their mission, which was to secure the port in Umm Qasr, the importance of which is evident when you consider that it's one of three main ports in the entire country. Once the port was secure, an engineer company moved in and swept the area for mines and any other explosives. Within a matter of days, in fact, before Echo Company had even reached its next mission, the port was up and running, and humanitarian aid was rolling into Iraq.

Echo Company ended the day of fighting in the vicinity of the original destination, although they were oriented exactly 180 degrees from it. That's the essence of fog and friction. Rarely are circumstances more unexpected than what

those Marines fought through that day, mostly because they didn't expect to fight that day. But the *Warfighting* philosophy held true. It was written more as a belief system for the battlefield, and each Marine held on to each principle and upheld the legacy of all the riflemen who fought before them.

Several days later, the men of Echo Company picked up a mission that would involve them in one of the war's most publicized events. They had moved on to Nasiriyah in a standard movement to contact after having completed the task of transporting an additional three hundred enemy prisoners of war safely down to holding locations in Umm Qasr. Once there, they were told to stage what would appear to the Iraqis to be a major assault just west of the hospital in town. Fifteen amtracs and three hundred Marines poured into position around the Fedayeen (Arab guerrillas who operate mainly against Israel, or in this case, Israeli supporters) headquarters under cover of

Lance Corporal Rodney Eric Brin breaks open a shed door in a cement factory during a mission. He is second team leader of the 3rd Squad of Beowulf, the regimental reserve force for Regimental Combat Team 2, responsible for myriad tasks, from security and sustainment operations to setting up snap vehicle control points.

darkness and secured a major intersection and opened the road through town. That enabled the next company to secure the home of a Ba'ath Party senior official and the next company after that one to secure a bridge crossing the Euphrates River.

Assuming that a major assault had begun, Iraqi forces scattered to position in what would have been nothing short of a futile attempt at defense. Then the helicopters carrying Force Recon Marines flew directly over the heads of Echo Company. Landing with relatively little resistance, they stormed the nearby hospital using only their night-vision equipment, and shortly before dawn, the commanding officers received calls over the radio that the objective had been safely accomplished. That objective was the rescue of Private Jessica Lynch.

A few moments later, Echo Company was instructed to secure the hospital and search for any other prisoners. What they found was an empty building. During the night raid a few hours earlier, every Iraqi soldier inside had abandoned his position in response to the American forces outside. None returned. They had all been captured or killed, or made the decision to desert. All that was left were uniforms, terrain maps, and a general's vehicle, which were quickly confiscated.

Pushing North to Baghdad

Along the push to Baghdad, the 3rd Battalion, 4th Marine Division (3/4), led by Lieutenant Colonel B. P. McCoy, was sent in to Al Kut to clear up a few trouble spots. The original plan was for all the Marine units in the area to join up north of the city and make the final run to Baghdad together. But the remaining Fedayeen and Republican Guard soldiers in Al Kut posed a great risk of attacking from the rear as soon as the Marines pulled out. So the 3/4 got the call to make sure that didn't happen.

As they reached the outskirts of town on April 3, 2003, the lead tank unit was passing by a stand of palm trees when an ambush broke out. About forty Iraqis were dug into fighting holes, and they were doing everything possible to exploit their advantage. But, like Lieutenant Colonel McCoy would later say, the Iraqis were the gang who couldn't shoot straight.

Dangerously close to the extreme front lines at the tip of the spear, Lieutenant Colonel McCoy found himself in his Humvee trapped behind tanks as the firestorm began. Marine Corps doctrine would say that the proper procedure is to return fire and get out of Dodge. With the tanks so close, the Humvee was boxed in. McCoy and his driver dove out and immediately began emptying their M16s in the direction of the Iraqis.

Realizing that their commanding officer was under heavy fire, Sergeant Major Dave Howell and his driver, Corporal Mark Evnin, added their rifles and a grenade launcher to the fight. Far outnumbered, the small group of Marines' only hope was to lay down as much fire as they could to suppress the enemy long enough to be joined by an infantry platoon. Lieutenant Colonel McCoy was a prime example of just how high the tradition of "every Marine a rifleman" truly does reach. Firing one grenade after another into the trees with reckless regard for himself, Corporal Evnin was hit in the pelvis with two rounds from a machine gun. He later died in the medevac helicopter.

It takes practice to be prepared to change course quickly in order to take advantage of circumstances as they happen. While it may seem obvious that Marines practice fighting wars, it's important to remember that the natural disorder of

Corporal James Key, with Headquarters Battalion, 1st Marine Regiment, 1st Regimental Combat Team, looks after a child who was separated from her father and brothers during a firefight between Iraqi soldiers and U.S. Marines outside An Nasiriyah.

the modern battlefield makes it impossible to plan for any possible situation. What the Corps does prepare for are possibilities.

The Marines of 3/4 had spent weeks in the scorching California desert training for battles just like this one. They had lobbed a thousand grenades, fired twice as many rounds down range, and lain flat on their bellies for hours on end in the 120-degree sand. They were ready. So when three amtracs full of infantry riflemen arrived and the ramps on the back dropped, their jobs were almost a matter of reflex.

The Iraqis abandoned their positions and ran, demoralized by the Marines' willingness to give all if necessary and

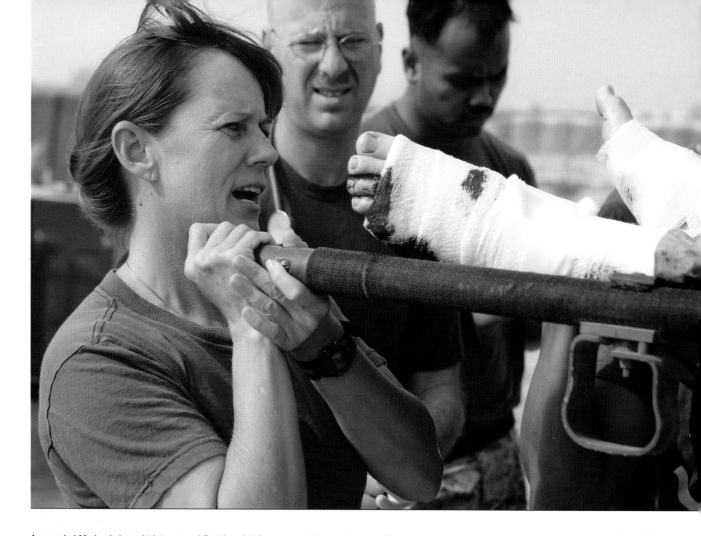

A wounded Marine is brought into a naval fleet hospital for treatment. The medical facilities can accommodate up to three hundred wounded and has full surgical operation capability.

fight down to the bayonet. All the while, the entire infantry platoon was steadily advancing, one small fire team at a time. Emphasizing Lieutenant Colonel McCoy's point about the Iraqis' inability to shoot, Corporal Evnin was the only American to die at Al Kut. Most likely the shots that hit him weren't aimed at him; rather, they were just part of the barrage. It was his dedication to the Corps and his selflessness that put him in their path.

Only a few days later, the 3/4 would find itself at the southeastern edge of Baghdad. McCoy's men were preparing the charge. The Fedayeen were fighting in small groups from

Marines of Echo Company, Battalion Landing Team, 2nd Battalion, 2nd Marines, 24th Marine Expeditionary Unit (Special Operations Capable), secured the town of Qualatsukar during Operation Iraqi Freedom. The mission was to tear down and remove Ba'ath party symbols and to collect and destroy weapons caches. Many photographs and other likenesses of Saddam Hussein were piled up and burned.

Sergeant Kent D. Padmore, guard chief for Fallujah's Civil-Military Operations Center's Entry Control Point 7, directs a crowd of local residents and children during a toy giveaway outside the center. U.S. Marines and Iraqi police distribute clothes and toys to local children outside the center every week, while local and military officials inside issue compensation payments and brainstorm ideas to rebuild the city's infrastructure.

rooftops and other strategic spots. Cobras were overhead and firing in every direction. And the Marines were pressing forward toward Diyala Bridge, the only thing left between them and Baghdad.

As they were retreating into the city, the Iraqis blew out an entire span of the main bridge and a hole in the footbridge beside it. The Marines pulled back so their engineers could figure out a way to cross. Their solution was to span the four-foot gap with an expanse of metal strong enough to hold a couple of Marines at a time. The tanks and other armored vehicles would have to wait.

For most of the next morning, the Marines traded fire with Republican Guard soldiers from one side of the bridge to the other. Both forces were lobbing mortar shells at each other. The Marines added some heavy artillery as well. The last two mortar rounds they fired were just smoke to provide cover as Kilo Company

Marines listen while local women tell of torture and killings under Saddam's dictatorship.

83

A Marine with Company K, 3rd Battalion, 25th Marine Regiment, and a soldier with the Iraq Intervention Force check out a suspicious vehicle while on patrol.

A hospital corpsman from Company I, 3rd Battalion, 25th Marines attends to an injured Iraqi soldier after an attack by insurgents who disrupted civilians receiving money from multinational forces. The attack damaged a bridge and caused more than forty wounded and one killed from multinational forces and eight civilian casualties.

bring in the vehicles. As they began to rumble farther into town, it became evident that the worst of the fight was well behind them. It turned into more of a parade than a march. Iraqi citizens were lining the streets clapping, cheering, and thanking the Marines.

Lieutenant Colonel McCoy and the rest of the 3/4 were ordered to the Palestine Hotel. In the square next to the hotel, Iraqis were gathering in an impromptu celebration. Before long, they began trying to knock down the statue of Saddam Hussein in the center of the square. After several unsuccessful attempts, many of them begged the Marines for help. Having fought valiantly over the course of several days, Lieutenant Colonel McCoy's men were rewarded by unintentionally creating the single most iconic image of the war. It was their M88 tank retriever that pulled down the statue as the world watched.

Lieutenant Colonel McCoy's pride in his Marines is evident. He reminds us all that every war comes down to last year's high school seniors. It's up to them to close the last three hundred yards between them and the enemy. And they never fail to do so. In his words, "It's humbling to be in their presence."

The Marines foster an orderly environment so they can function within the disorderly atmosphere of battle. Decisions made in the heat of the moment happen in fractions of a second, and not everyone is cut out to do that. But it is precisely what Marines train for. Decentralized decision making and individual abilities are held in high esteem within the Corps. Even the most junior Marines are expected to show a great deal of leadership, particularly when compared to their counterparts in other military organizations.

charged forward with the bridge patch. Once the patch was in place, they rushed over the bridge and into the city. So, after having come ashore aboard amphibious artillery vehicles and making the long trek north with amtracs, trucks, and tanks, the gleaming point of the spear entered Baghdad on foot.

It didn't take long for the enemy fire to die down. The mighty Republican Guard soldiers had abandoned their positions yet again. Marine engineers set up pontoon bridges to

Lance Corporal Jacob L. Hassell, a rifleman with Company B, 1st Battalion, 8th Marine Regiment, Regimental Combat Team 7, takes a moment to sit down after intense fighting in Fallujah during Operation Al Fajr.

Insurgents and Urban Warfare — Maneuvering in the Narrow Streets

Shortly after the first twenty-two days of fighting came to a close, a new problem became violently clear: Insurgents were bound and determined to drive U.S. and coalition forces from their country. Their tactics varied depending on any number of factors, including which cleric they're following—usually someone with iconic status—or what region they're from, due to regional history and the level of importance of recent and ancient ancestors within the government of Iraq.

Warfare doesn't get any more chaotic and disorderly than if you're fighting hundreds of detached bands of insurgents who all want the same things for different reasons. Their strategies range from improvised explosive devices (IEDs) to outright violations of Geneva Convention policies that govern guerrilla forces. Additionally, they've used kidnappings, hostage-takings, hijackings, and shooting, all with very little regard for the lives of their fellow countrymen.

As of January 2006, Marines were still heavily involved in fighting the insurgency in Iraq. This type of fighting is anything but traditional. Marines fanned out in areas known to harbor insurgents and sought them out, knocking on doors

This is what remains following a three-hour firefight between the Marines of 3rd Platoon, 2nd Battalion, 2nd Marine Regiment, and a cell of insurgents in Al Anbar Province. The Marines killed and wounded most of the insurgents in the house, which severely hurt the insurgent cells in the area.

Fellow Marines with 4th Squad, Military Police Detachment, and friends gather around to pay their last respects to Lance Corporal Marc L. Tucker, a motor transportation operator augmented as a military policeman, MP Detachment, Combat Logistics Battalion 2, 2nd Force Service Support Group (Forward). Tucker was attached to 4th Squad, MP Detachment, and deployed to Iraq to provide security for the explosive ordnance disposal team, recovery missions, engineer crater repair missions, and convoys. During the memorial service, Tucker's friends talked about how he influenced and touched each one of their lives. Most of the Marines spoke of the great amount of respect and love they have for their "brother."

and searching every alley. All the while, every hair on their necks was standing at attention, for they never knew where the next bullet would come from.

To be successful, the insurgents used nontraditional techniques because they didn't have the same capabilities of the coalition forces they were fighting. Generally, they used IEDs to target supply chains and security forces. An IED could be homemade or manu-

A wounded Marine is carried onto a CH-46 from Marine Medium Helicopter Squadron 364. The unit, also called "Purple Foxes," flies casualty evacuation (CASEVAC) missions in support of the 2nd Marine Expeditionary Force (Forward) CASEVAC team. The team responds to calls from throughout the Al Anbar Province, flying into the face of danger to extract wounded Marines, soldiers, and civilians.

factured from discarded Iraqi artillery, in which case the usual choice was a 155mm shell rigged with plastic explosives. However, as the insurgents became more sophisticated, they made the bombs larger and with shaped charges, which allowed the blasts to be focused. Regardless of how they were made, IEDs were usually placed along roadsides in piles of garbage or buried in the ground, or, in some cases, placed inside dead animals.

This being the case, it's easy to see how difficult it can be for Marines to train to spot something that's not all that out of place. Patrols must rely on instinct and caution because they never know what might blow up next. Certainly IEDs claimed entirely too many U.S. Marines during the second Gulf War, not to mention troops from the other coalition forces. But as more forces patrol the hotbeds of insurgent activity, they are becoming more adept at spotting them.

Second only to roadside IEDs are suicide bombers, who wreak more havoc among civilians than the Marines and other coalition forces ever do. While the insurgents can claim the actual targets to be legitimate, the simple fact is that police stations, security service recruiting stations, and U.S. convoys are often located in populated areas.

Lance Corporal Paul Jones, advanced field artillery tactical data system operator and sentry on the combat operations center (COC) guard force, speaks over the radio to his fellow sentries. Jones is well known by all Marines, sailors, and soldiers who work at the COC. That is because they cannot get past Jones without a holler and a greeting of the day.

Car bombs are the weapon of choice for most suicide bombs. They're referred to as vehicle-borne IEDs, and they're practically impossible to defend against. They disguise themselves as noncombatants, and they hide hundreds, sometimes

An Iraqi man who was held captive and beaten by insurgents has welts and lacerations across his back and arms from being tortured with electricity. The man was hung by his feet, his head was dipped in water, and he was then tortured with electric shock. He and three others were rescued by Iraqi Security Forces and Marines from 3rd Battalion, 2nd Marine Regiment, who discovered an insurgent torture chamber in the city of Karabilah, Iraq, during Operation Romhe. The Marines entered a building believed to be a car bomb factory and found these men. The four Iraqis received immediate first aid and were transported to a medical facility for further treatment and recovery. Operation Romhe's mission was to destroy strongholds held by insurgents in Karabilah. The Marines of 2nd Marine Division conducted counterinsurgency operations with Iraqi Security Forces to isolate and neutralize insurgents, to support the continued development of Iraqi Security Forces, and to support Iraqi reconstruction and democratic elections to create a secure environment that enables Iraqi self-reliance and self-governance.

Corporal Timothy Culbertson, a Marine manning Fallujah's Entry Control Point-One "Alpha," escorts an insurgent Iraqi policeman. Iraqi Security Forces and Marines with 1st Battalion, 6th Marine Regiment, apprehended a total of four suspected terrorists for weapons possession, emplacing roadside bombs, and possible involvement in a nearby firefight.

thousands, of pounds of explosives. Early in the war, Iraqis primarily used junker cars as bombing vehicles. As soon as they realized Americans had caught on to this, they began using brand-new Mercedes.

These deceptive practices place Marines on patrol in an unenviable position. How do you know if the truck approaching is full of produce, the way it appears to be, or if what's visible is hiding enough firepower to crumble an entire city block? Do you shoot and risk killing unarmed civilians, or do you do nothing and fall victim to a blatant war crime?

Perfidy is the practice of combatants disguising themselves as noncombatants, and it's a violation of the Geneva Convention. It's also one of the insurgents' favorite tactics.

Marines check a vehicle and its passengers at a checkpoint to find insurgents and weapons.

Lance Corporal Joe P. Lariccia (left) and First Lieutenant Adam W. Burch, both with 5th Mobile Assault Platoon, Company W, 1st Battalion, 5th Marine Regiment, have their weapons at the ready and post security for their comrades during a mission in Ramadi. The platoon's warriors conducted a presence patrol in the southern part of the city in an effort to uncover insurgent activity and deter them from operating. The platoon was engaged by an enemy sniper and hit an improvised explosive device during the operation. No one was hurt, and no vehicles were damaged.

Having held themselves to a higher standard for so long, Marines don't have the luxury of firing at will. One wrong, or even questionable, move and the entire world scrutinizes the whole of the Corps. Such an incident occurred on November 13, 2004, after an intense firefight in one of Fallujah's many mosques that the guerrilla fighters were using as a hideout. A Marine was videotaped shooting and killing an unarmed alleged insurgent. Given the insurgents' well-known tactic of playing dead and then attacking, that Marine was justifiably found not guilty of manslaughter in a military court. Additional insurgent tactics have involved surrendering and

Team leader Corporal Patrick M. Dunn, of 1st Squad, 1st Platoon, Company A, 1st Battalion, 5th Marine Regiment, uses a crowbar to bash the lock off a door to a building he and his Marines need to search. His squad's mission is to reach the rooftop and serve as lookouts for other Marines patrolling the streets below. Marines with Company A patrolled the busy marketplace in an effort to become more familiar with their area of operations and make their presence known to the local populace. The Marines also searched several buildings and a nearby mosque for weapons caches and insurgents. The three-hour patrol ended with the Marines returning empty-handed to their base camp at Hurricane Point.

Weapons at the ready, two Marines from Bravo Company, Battalion Landing Team (BLT), 1st Battalion, 6th Marines, enter a building during Operation Cadillac Ranch, a cordon-and-search operation in Afghanistan's Oruzgan Province. BLT 1/6 is the ground combat element of the 22nd Marine Expeditionary Unit (Special Operations Capable).

then attacking, and even rigging the dead or wounded with bombs. It's not easy to fight a force with so little regard for any human life.

True to their disregard for human life, insurgents often fired mortars or rockets at coalition targets from heavily populated areas. Their thinking was correct, as U.S. forces discourage counterfire into urban developments. So, as inaccurate as these guerrilla shooters were, there was little moti-

A Marine with Company A, 1st Battalion, 5th Marine Regiment, stands guard outside a house while the rest of his squad searches for weapons and enemies. This raid was one of many operations 1/5 did to help incoming 3rd Battalion, 7th Marine Regiment, get accustomed to the area.

Lance Corporal Darin Emde surveys a mountain in Afghanistan's Oruzgan Province for Taliban snipers firing upon him and his fellow Marines in Charlie Company, Battalion Landing Team, 1st Battalion, 6th Marines. BLT 1/6 was conducting Operation Asbury Park.

ation for them to stop, especially since these strikes did occasionally hit their mark.

There are still more tactics that Marines must try to figure out on a daily basis. For example, helicopters have been regular targets of RPGs and heat-seeking shoulder-fired missiles. An insurgent will typically lie in wait until a helicopter passes over and then take aim at its tail end. Since the enemy is not engaging them from the front, helicopter pilots defend themselves and their aircraft by flying at low altitudes and a high rate of speed. Given the Marine air mission of close-air support, this is a technique that Marine pilots are very comfortable with.

Insurgents in Afghanistan

Don't think that Marines only battled these forces in Iraq. On August 18, 2005, the Marines of Echo Company, 2nd Battalion, 3rd Marine Regiment were ambushed at the conclusion of a nine-day mission in the Korengal Valley, Afghanistan. Echo Company had been taking part in a security and stabilization operation in the valley, an area that was no stranger to attacks such as this on coalition forces.

They were there as a show of force and solidarity for upcoming elections in the region. This platoon's specific mission was to regulate traffic in and out of the area. Having completed their mission, the men were on their way back to base and were reinforced with machine guns and Afghan National Army soldiers. The platoon was traveling in a tactical formation, two kilometers away from its extraction point, when it came under fire. The ambush happened at sundown as the Marines made their way through the village of Taleban.

The insurgents used rocket-propelled grenades and small arms, and according to the Marines under attack, those weapons

Marines of Charlie Company, Battalion Landing Team, 1st Battalion, 6th Marines, thread their way through a narrow village alley in Afghanistan's Oruzgan Province in their search for weapons caches and anticoalition fighters during Operation Thunder Road.

First Sergeant Ernest Hoopi, first sergeant for Charlie Company, Battalion Landing Team, 1st Battalion, 6th Marines, trudges over rough Afghan terrain carrying Lance Corporal James Wood. Moments earlier, Wood was shot in the leg by anticoalition militia in central Afghanistan during an engagement with elements of the 22nd Marine Expeditionary Unit.

were in no short supply. The men of Echo Company immediately shed their packs and dove for cover. Talk to any Marines who have never been in a firefight, and every one of them will tell you the same thing: that he hopes that when the day comes his training will kick in and he'll react accordingly. That's exactly what Echo Company did that evening. They were returning fire from both sides of the road, but they may as well have still been standing out in the open. With enemies shooting at them from every possible angle, they were completely exposed.

In addition to the RPGs and small arms fire, mortar shells began dropping all around them. Unlike previous attacks in the area, these insurgents were using advanced ambush attacks. Firing from three positions, they used a pile of rocks placed in the middle of the road to find their distance and measure their shots. Then, after

the Marines' attention had been directed to the rear, the insurgent began to fire at the front from ground level. The firefight lasted fo an hour, but when it was over, it was the Marines who counted thre dead insurgents and recovered several sources of intelligence.

Fallujah

For a city that became almost a pilgrimage destination fo insurgents who wanted to martyr themselves, Fallujah wa one of the most peaceful areas of Iraq early on in the wa Signs of trouble began shortly after Saddam Hussein's fa from power. The city's new mayor, Taha Bidayi Hamed although chosen by local tribal leaders, was pro-American Assisted by U.S.-led occupants, local Iraqis established th Fallujah Protection Force to help fight the rising resistance.

Marines from the Force Reconnaissance platoon of the 22nd Marine Expeditionary Unit (Special Operations Capable), mounted on a vehicle, join Marines from the Battalion Reconnaissance platoon of Battalion Landing Team, 1st Battalion, 6th Marines, and Afghan National Army troops in a patrol near Dey Chopan, Afghanistan, during Operation Asbury Park.

In March 2004, the Marines received control of Fallujah from the 82nd Airborne and the 3rd Cavalry, as a result of which they controlled the entire Al Anbar province. But by the end of the month, unrest among the Iraqis would turn to outright violence.

On March 31, 2004, four employees of Blackwater USA, serving as private military contractors, were dragged from their vehicle and killed. Not satisfied that their point had been made, the militants then mutilated and burned the Americans' bodies. They beat and dragged the corpses behind their vehicles and finally hanged them above a bridge crossing the Euphrates River. These acts were well publicized after journalists broadcast video footage of them worldwide.

Early in April 2004, Marines surrounded the city and made an attempt to capture the people responsible for the four American deaths. The endeavor, dubbed Operation Vigilant Resolve, was meant to regain control of Fallujah. About forty Marines died in the action, and a few days later, a unilateral truce was declared to allow for humanitarian supplies to reach the city. By the terms of the truce, the Marines had to pull back from the city.

The insurgents took the opportunity to build their supply of weapons; many were even found hidden in the humanitarian supply trucks entering the city. Control of the city had been handed back over to the Iraqis under shaky terms. The new leader, General Muhammed Latif, then formed a thousand-man force called the Fallujah Brigade. Even General Latif acknowledged that many of those men were probably insurgents themselves. Yet the terms of cease-fire stated that Fallujah was to become secure for coalition forces, and mortar and RPG attacks on U.S. bases were to stop.

Perched behind a machine gun in a UH-1N Huey helicopter, Staff Sergeant Mark J. Covill, a crew chief with Marine Light Attack Helicopter (HMLA) Squadron 775, surveys the area around a farm near Camp Taqaddum, Iraq, during a reconnaissance patrol. The Marines of HMLA 775, a reserve squadron based in Camp Pendleton, California, and Johnstown, Pennsylvania, provide security for 1st Force Service Support Group convoys moving supplies throughout the Al Anbar Province of Iraq. The pilots use bird's-eye view and firepower to try to spot and eliminate possible roadside explosives and ambushes before a convoy reaches them.

Tensions grew throughout the summer. A traffic control point (TCP) had been established on the eastern side of the city, and it was manned twenty-four hours a day by a platoon of Marines and Iraqi National Guardsmen. For weeks on end, the TCP was the subject of almost daily firefights. By midsummer, Fallujah had deteriorated to a state of lawlessness that was controlled by the mujahideen (a military force of Muslim guerrilla warriors engaged in a jihad) and warlords. The Fallujah Brigade had only succeeded in hastening the process of turning the city into a danger zone for all coalition troops.

On October 14, 2004, CNN aired a report from a young Marine officer, First Lieutenant Lyle Gilbert, that said the United States had begun the impending assault on Fallujah. Within hours, Pentagon reporters had determined that the report was indeed false. Several weeks later, unnamed Pentagon officials admitted that the Marine's announcement was meant to determine the reactio of insurgents who thought an attack was imminent.

Then, on November 8, 2004, the fight for Fallujah begar American forces consisted of six combined battalions of arm soldiers and Marines. They found out very quickly how bus the rebel forces had been in the six months since the Marine had pulled back. Mouse holes had been cut into walls so th insurgents could move from one building complex to anothe without detection. They had dispersed large caches o weapons throughout the city, and the entire town seemed t be booby-trapped with IEDs.

The plan was to move from the north and push sout quickly. The 3rd Battalion, 1st Marines (3/1) was to take th Jolan neighborhood in the northwestern area of the city. had become the epicenter of activity for anyone with a grudg

The Marines of Firepower Control Team 1 (FCT 1), 3rd Platoon, 2nd Air Naval Gunfire Liaison Company (ANGLICO), Regimental Combat Team (RCT) 7, conduct a "talk in," directing an aircraft on an armed reconnaissance mission over potential targets from a rooftop in Haditha, Iraq. ANGLICO Marines incorporated fixed- and rotary-wing assets in the fight during Operation River Blitz. They were able to drop five-hundred-pound bombs and call in a barrage from an AC-130 Gunship.

gainst American and coalition troops. Repeated warnings ad been made for the city to be evacuated, so there was no oubt that anyone left was there solely to kill.

Ask any Marine what the most significant battle of the arly twenty-first century was, and he or she will tell you allujah. It stretched out for more than two weeks. The fight as confusing, loud, and exhausting, and it emphasized the mportance of the 360-degree patrol tactics employed by Marine fire teams.

One of the reasons why the insurgents had dispersed heir weapons caches around the city was so they could travel ghtly. While a Marine considers his rifle an extension of imself, his enemy had no such attachment to his own eapon. With so many to choose from, the insurgents would arry a weapon as long as it was useful to him. Once a rifle as out of ammunition, or if the insurgent needed something

with more firepower, all he needed to do was pick something new from the stack. When it came time to change position, none of them carried a rifle along; they would simply pick up a new one when they got there.

The stories from the fight for Fallujah, like most Marine Corps battles, demonstrate the Marines' pledge of honor, courage, and commitment. On the third day of the battle, a fire team from Alpha Company, 1st Battalion, 8th Marines was out on a search-and-destroy mission. They were going house to house rooting out insurgents wherever they found them. At one house, shortly after sunrise, the Marines were pinned down on a rooftop by snipers shooting from windows of buildings above them. The only thing protecting them from the bullets was a low wall and a lot of luck. Finally, one of the Marines spotted a sniper's position and called it out to the others. Lying flat on his back, one of the Alpha Company

Marines with Company I, 3rd Battalion, 25th Marines watch as a bomb called in by tactical air control party chief Sergeant Aaron J. Maxwell successfully hits its target.

Lance Corporal Wyatt Schertenleib and Lance Corporal Adam Smith of the 24th Marine Expeditionary Unit (MEU) help secure a concertina-wire barrier in a canal, upstream from a recently destroyed bridge in Lutafiyah, Iraq. They set up the wire to prevent possible floating improvised explosive devices from hampering the MEU's bridge reconstruction efforts. The bridge was severely damaged in repeated attacks by insurgents. Both Schertenleib and Smith are combat engineers with Engineer Detachment, MEU Service Support Group 24. The 24th MEU continued to conduct security and stability operations in northern Babil Province.

Marines loaded his M230 grenade launcher and, from 300 yards away, took out the sniper with a perfect shot he fired blindly. Another Marine had armed his shoulder-fired AT4 antiarmor missile launcher, but he wouldn't have to waste his shot to clear hi position safely. There was a second sniper and once the team had his position figured out, they hatched a plan. On the count of three, two of them sat up and released a spray of bullets. A split second later, the AT4 spat out its missile, and like the grenade before it hit the target dead-on. Three smoke grenades later, the fire team left the rooftop unscathed to rejoin their platoon.

Four days into the battle, the Marine were ready to cross Highway 10, the major east/west route through the heart of Fallujah, on their push south. One platoon took the opportunity to advance at night because the insurgents wouldn't engage

These Marines get some much-needed rest during intense fighting that took place over several days in Fallujah. After the Marines emplaced security, they rotated riflemen so the security personnel could rest before moving back out to continue combat operations.

them after dark. The Marines were able to set up a fighting position in a convenience store that took the insurgents completely by surprise the next morning. The platoon had organized for a long fight. The commanding officer (CO) had established a system of one team up and fighting while two were in the basement of the store resting and cleaning their weapons.

Eventually, the rebel forces locked onto the Americans' position and were able to surround them from the west, south, and east. An insurgent sniper worked his way into an advantageous angle that cleared several shots. With the first, he grazed the helmet of one Marine who was dragged out of the fight. His replacement was then shot in the head through his helmet. He was then dragged from the fight and ended up surviving. The machine gunner was hit next, but he refused medical assistance until he was able to get off twenty

to thirty rounds back at the sniper. Not surprisingly, the sniping stopped.

At that point, the Marines were ordered to move out and link up with the rest of the platoon. There was no back door to the convenience store, and the danger out front was far too great for the Marines to exit there. The CO instructed an engineer to rig one of the walls with C4 explosives, which enabled them to go out fighting and make their way toward an alley. They got out of the building safely, but they encountered yet another firefight once they reached their destination. The military term for what these men encountered that day is "close combat." When it gets as close as it was in Fallujah, however, "point-blank combat" is probably more accurate.

Kilo Company, 3rd Battalion, 1st Marines found out just how point-blank it could get. During another search-and-destroy mission, two Marines entered a house. They made

Corporal Matt Morrish, team leader, 2nd Platoon, Company B, 1st Battalion, 23rd Marines, displays some holiday cheer on his helmet at his observation post in the field around Ar Ramadi, Iraq. From the company's leadership on down, the unit pulled together on Christmas Day to deliver some hot holiday chow and mail to the Marines pulling sentry duty in the field near one of Iraq's main highways.

Corporal Carlos A. Felix Jr., a squad leader with 1st Platoon, Charlie Company, 1st Battalion, 7th Marine Regiment, Regimental Combat Team (RCT) 7, enjoys a few moments of downtime with his squad as they break open meals, ready to eat (MREs) while taking cover in a burned-out hotel in Haqlaniyah, Iraq. In this building, Marines took machine gun fire from the island across the river.

rifles are lined up, dug into the ground, and displayed with boots, helmets, and dog tags, serving as a representation of four fallen Marines from Combat Service Support Company 113, Combat Service Support Battalion 1, 1st Force Service Support Group, during a memorial service at Camp Taqaddum, Iraq. Hundreds of Marines attended the memorial service of Staff Sergeant David G. Ries, Corporal Joshua D. Palmer, Lance Corporal Jeffrey Lam, and Lance Corporal Thomas J. Zapp. All four Marines died November 8, 2004—Ries and Zapp due to enemy action in the Al Anbar Province of Iraq, and Palmer and Lam while building a fighting position near the Fallujah peninsula. The bulldozer Palmer was operating fell into the Euphrates River after the ground gave way. "Each of them knew the risks and still answered the call," said Lieutenant Colonel Kurt A. Kempster, Combat Service Support Battalion 1's commanding officer, during the service. "They volunteered to serve their country and made the ultimate sacrifice so others less fortunate could experience the freedoms we all enjoy."

their way back to a bathroom door, and when they kicked it down, they discovered an insurgent who had been lying in wait. Literally right inside the door, he took aim but missed. Neither one of the Marines missed, but the gunfire alerted other insurgents in the house to their presence. They unloaded from the rooftop through skylights.

A rescue team went in, and they too were met with hails of fire from AK-47s, as well as a few grenades. First Sergeant Brad Kasal led the rescue mission, and on the way into the house, he grabbed Private First Class Alexander Nicoll to go with him. Once inside, there was no time to get their bearings. The insurgents were intent on fighting to the death, and they got right down to business. One pointed his AK-47 right at Kasal. He fired and missed. Kasal proved to be a much better shot. What he didn't know was that there was another insurgent behind them on the steps to the second floor. He let fly with a hail of automatic

gunfire and hit both Kasal and Nicoll in the legs. As he was going down, Kasal saw a grenade rolling toward them. Acting purely on instinct, he shielded Nicoll's body with his own. Kasal's back absorbed the blast. His body armor and helmet took the rest, which is why he survived. In total he was hit five times in his right leg, once in the right foot, and once in the buttocks.

Dizzy from the force of the blast and now also bleeding from shrapnel wounds to the shoulders, legs, and back, Kasal still managed to get out his 9mm pistol. He lay on the floor, still shielding Nicoll, ready to hold off the insurgents even though he was fading in and out of consciousness as he lost 60 percent of his blood. It took a half-hour, but support arrived and pulled the Marines out. Later, Marines loaded a satchel with twenty pounds of C4 and leveled the house.

The Corps would much rather eliminate the enemy than take a chance that the enemy may return. Usually, the

Captain Jody White, Company C commander, 1st Battalion, 6th Marine Regiment, talks on the radio outside a home during Operation Hard Knock. The battalion's Marines and Iraqi Security Forces blocked off a sector of northwestern Fallujah to search dozens of houses for weapons and to gather census information on the populace.

Marines accomplish this goal with a great show of force. The message is clear to an enemy: Take one of ours and we'll take as many of yours as we can at once. When Lima Company, 3rd Battalion, 1st Marines was clearing houses in the southwest section of town, it had already lost several of its own in Jolan. The 1st Platoon encountered an insurgent after they thought the area was all clear. He ran into a courtyard and the platoon all gathered at the wall to lob in grenades. Sergeant Ben Connor entered the courtyard to confirm that the insurgent was dead. Passing a window, he was discovered by a second rebel, who sprayed him with gunfire from his AK-47, hitting Connor in the arm. He called to his unit that he needed cover fire to make his way out. As soon as Lance Corporal Hanks appeared in an opening in the wall, the insurgent near Connor fired his machine gun. A round hit Hanks in the head, killing him. Sergeant Connor made his way out, and the Marines responded with an M1A1 tank. Not long after, a bulldozer appeared and leveled the wreckage

that was left. Again, Marines didn't leave the enemy an opportunity to return.

The Marines were surprised by how organized and skilled the force was that they faced in Fallujah. For example, rather than just firing at the Marines' chests, the insurgents knew that they could circumvent any body armor by aiming at their faces. American military officials were hoping to capture Abu Musab al-Zarqawi (head of al Qaeda operations in Iraq) in the fight for Fallujah. Instead, they discovered that he had no intention of sticking around for a battle. But the Marines did retake control of the town, and for that, they were very proud of themselves. Best-guess estimates were in the range of two thousand insurgents killed to the ninety Americans who died. Later, intercepted cell phone conversations revealed a great deal of surprise from the insurgents who complained about how quickly the Marines were adapting to their tactics and that they seemed to be everywhere. One Marine officer invoked the famous line from Iwo Jima when he said, "Uncommon valor is still a common virtue." That alone is an indication of the importance the Corps placed on the fight for Fallujah. But the spirit of the Corps was summed up by one officer's response when asked how so many acts of bravery can take place on the same battlefield. He quoted a book he had recently read: "The opposite of fear isn't courage. The opposite of fear is love."

No Matter How It's Fought, War Makes Angels

Military culture is full of acronyms. Every piece of equipment and every action is abbreviated in some way or another. But in a fitting tribute to fallen Marines, no acronym is used by those who must retrieve them from the battlefield. The fallen are simply referred to as Angels. The Corps has many stories of legendary Marines, but there are none more honored than those who make the ultimate sacrifice for the country they love.

For years, the Marine Corps didn't have an official Mortuary Affairs MOS. They did have a few Marines trained to do the job in Iraq for Desert Storm (January to February 1991), but it was not pursued. The decision to reinstate the unit was made early in 2003 during the buildup to the second Gulf War. After all, Marines take great pride in caring for their own, and you can bet that was the main reason for the decision. The Marines believed that it's only proper for another Marine to ensure that those who die in battle receive the respect that they've earned.

Serving in the Marine reserves, Sergeant Ernest Claiborne had already seen his fair share of death and destruction in his full-time job with the City of Hampton, Georgia, police department. Prior to that career, however, he spent eight and a half years on active duty with the Marines. In February 2005, Sergeant Claiborne was called to return to active duty

Sergeant Daniel Kachmar, 2nd Squad leader, 4th Platoon, Company A, 1st Battalion, 6th Marine Regiment, searches for weapons inside a home during Operation Hard Knock. Company A Marines searched dozens of houses throughout a small township outside Fallujah, looking for weapons, explosives, and insurgent activity. The Marines apprehended one suspected insurgent supporter.

FLO

Private Sayf Jamel Mahdy, an Iraqi soldier teaching alongside 1st Battalion, 6th Marine Regiment's Iraqi Security Forces training cadre, leads his fellow soldiers during marksmanship training exercises. The personnel of 1/6 trained Iraqi personnel on topics such as first aid in combat, infantry tactics, and convoy driving skills. Iraqi forces were fully integrated into every operation that the battalion's Marines and sailors conducted in and around the city of Fallujah.

and was sent with a Mortuary Affairs unit to Al Taqaddam (TQ), due west of Baghdad. Once there, Claiborne's lieutenant colonel and First Sergeant Jamie Karnes nominated him to serve as the operations chief. In that role, he was responsible for planning the operations to retrieve the fallen Marines when they received an "incoming Angels" call. The difficulty with many of those calls is that it's not uncommon for incoming rounds to show up at the same time.

It was First Sergeant Karnes' second tour with Mortuary Affairs. A career reservist, Karnes' full-time job is as a special agent with the Georgia Bureau of Investigation, a position he has held since February 2001. Interestingly, Karnes spent the first fourteen years of his reservist career without being activated. Then, in a twist of fate that for some reason only seems capable in the military, he was activated for the first time shortly after he got married. In March 2003, his

unit from Marietta, Georgia, was lumped together with detachments from several other reserve forces to form a group of three hundred Marines that became the Mortuary Affairs Company. Karnes was in charge of attaching his men to other units so they would be present to collect fallen Marines and get them transported back down to the main facility in Doha, Qatar. Even though it was located in a remote tent city a few miles off the main road, the camp was the subject of several missile strikes. From their vantage point, Karnes remembers seeing rounds impacting around Kuwait, the city of Doha, and of course his own camp.

Two years later, Karnes returned to Iraq with Sergeant Claiborne and the rest of the Marines attached to the Mortuary Affairs Company. They had been on the ground for barely six hours when they got their first call. At thirty-two, Sergeant Claiborne was the fourth-oldest Marine in the unit. After eight and a half years of prior service, he and the other "old men" had pretty much seen it all. But when four mortar rounds landed in succession all around them, the eyes of the younger Marines with them were officially opened.

To the Marines, death is more than just the aftermath of a battle. Guys who were once jokesters fall silent. Men who may have just sent a letter to their family will now arrive home long before the letter ever does. So when Marines fall in battle, other Marines take good care of them. But it's not easy. Sergeant Claiborne remembers the day he and his men recovered a Marine whose twin brother served in the same company but a different platoon. They presented the surviving brother with his twin's flag and then allowed him to escort him home.

Because war doesn't stop to rest, those involved rarely get to. The same goes for the Marines of Mortuary Affairs. Running on three hours of sleep at most, these guys were fueled by the importance of what they did, and they were numbed by what they saw. Often, there was little more than dog tags to recover. Other times only a name tag, or worse. One of Sergeant Claiborne's own friends was recovered while he was there—a guy he had known from their days as boot Marines.

Mortuary Affairs has second overall priority for evacuation, which means they leave with the dead after the wounded and before the remaining Marines. This philosophy mirrors every other aspect of the Corps, and no Marine worth his dog tags would ever think of boarding a helicopter before his fallen brother or sister. During his second tour with the Mortuary Affairs Company, Sergeant Karnes was repeatedly touched when a fallen Marine was placed on board a C-130 for his or her final trip home.

A C-130 Hercules is a monster of a plane with a wingspan of over 132 feet. Its four propeller-driven engines make a lot of noise. But when the cargo it's meant to carry is a fallen soldier or Marine, it shuts down out of respect during the loading process. An American flag is hung from the top of the plane, and two columns are formed by all available personnel, one on either side of the plane facing inboard. A few Marines will take the transfer case holding the fallen Marine from the back of a truck and carry it gracefully and methodically across the tarmac

to the C-130. Once they place the case onboard the aircraft, they do an about-face and proceed to the ends of the columns, where they execute another about-face and fall in line.

During the boarding process, the flight crew turns on the white lights inside the plane's hold area for the benefit of those loading the transfer case. But once the transfer case is securely onboard and the columns have broken as the Marines return to their duty, the white lights go off and the green tactical lights inside the plane are turned back on. First Sergeant Karnes describes the moment as solemn, knowing that his hands will be among the last to have passed the legacy of that Marine on into the care of his or her family.

Mortuary Affairs Marines follow strict rules and time-honored traditions when handling the bodies of Marines who made the ultimate sacrifice. They don't stand over the remains, and they will not walk over them. They say that those are tasks left to friends and enemies. There's an old saying that you can judge a civilization by how they treat their children, their elderly, and their dead. Leave it to the Marines to be the most civilized of us all.

Marines with 2nd Platoon, Company W, 1st Battalion, 5th Marine Regiment, stop a man driving in a street in Ar Ramadi and search his car during a mission in the city. The Marines conduct proactive operations to encourage the citizens to move their trash cans off the streets and place them in the yards behind their homes. In 2005, the Iraqi government distributed new orange, industrial-size trash containers throughout the city for citizens to dispose of rubbish, but officials with the 1st Battalion, 5th Marines, suspected that insurgents would exploit them for terror and place improvised explosive devices in them.

Chapter 4

THE FUTURE OF THE CORPS
SECURING THE FUTURE OF OUR COUNTRY

Even with the success the Marines enjoyed in 2003 on their lightning-quick march into Baghdad, they can't seem to shake the fact that there will always be those who question their legitimacy. Every few years, it seems they have to answer questions about their supposed redundancy. The army's strategic concept has not changed much over the last sixty years. But every branch of the military is working toward deploying troops in an expeditionary manner. The army in particular is sending its units out in a much lighter structure that looks very much like a MAGTF. So the questions being asked are: Where does that leave the Marine Corps? Does the United States need a Marine Corps that's bigger than the armies of many other countries?

In short, the Marine Corps is a thriving organization that is now and will be for a long time to come extremely valuable to the United States for more than just beach landings. In fact, while the term "amphibious" is representative of one of the Marine Corps' greatest strengths, it has been used to box the Corps into a singular purpose in the eyes of some.

The true meaning of "amphibious" is much broader. Its origins are from classical Greek and mean to live "all around" or "on both sides"—in other words, on land and in water. Many people forget that the Marines don't just come ashore; they also have the unique ability to return to the sea after conducting operations on land. More than that, Marines have the experience necessary to use open water as more than a base; they treat it as maneuver space and can thus project power ashore anytime, anywhere.

Marines with 1st Platoon, Lima Company, Third Battalion, 25th Marines, roam the streets of Baghdad during Operation Sword.

Opposite: The Marines of Team 3, Detachment 4, 6th Civil Affairs Group (CAG), stand in Fallujah after meeting with local Iraqi community leaders. The purpose of the CAG is to connect with the local Iraqi community and government to promote good relations. The mission utilizes different teams throughout Al Anbar Province.

Traditionally, the Marines have focused on the world's littorals. But then the Marines captured an air field that was nowhere near a shoreline in Afghanistan in 2001. And in 2003, Marines formed one of the two main axes of advance on the march to Baghdad. Clearly, the strengths of the Corps extend well beyond beach landings. Plus, ever since Baghdad in 2003, the Marines have played one of the feature roles in the fight against insurgents.

These and many other examples point to the importance of responsiveness, flexibility, and adaptability on the battle-field. Each of those three qualities is a core strength of the Marines, who were previously only employed for landings. Those qualities will be required of all forces to meet the changing nature of battle. Indeed, the efforts in Afghanistan and Iraq brought the military's attention squarely to land forces. Without the boots on the ground, there can be no war termination, which is the successful transition from military action to peace.

Most military planners agree that future operations involving land forces will be expeditionary in nature. Clearly, this is a situation that the Marines will be very comfortable with, and one that the army is working hard to measure up to.

Sergeant Donald F. Lutz, a machine gunner with 2nd Platoon, Company K, 3rd Battalion, 1st Marine Regiment, positions himself on the roof of an abandoned building in Fallujah and sights down an alleyway to provide cover for his platoon, setting up a temporary base of operations. The following day, 3/1 conducted a tactical assault on a mosque in Fallujah with the support of air strikes and artillery. The mosque was a storage facility for weapons used by insurgents against multinational forces. The assault was part of Operation Al Fajr, an offensive by the Iraqi Security Forces and multinational forces designed to clear the restive city of Fallujah of the insurgents and terrorists who used the city as a safe haven for their brutal activities.

Lance Corporal Michael Hernandez, an infantryman with 4th Platoon, Company C, 1st Battalion, 6th Marine Regiment, and an Iraqi policeman determine which route to take next while patrolling the streets during Operation Hard Knock. Iraqi Security Forces and Marine personnel detained three suspected insurgent supporters and confiscated one hand grenade during this three-hour-long house-to-house search mission.

While the odds are good that the army will be successful, it's hard to argue with the viability of an organization that has specialized in expeditionary actions since its inception. So it may not be a matter of if the Marines will continue to have a role in securing the nation's interests, but rather how much more involved they will be.

Mirroring the expeditionary, out-in-front nature of the Corps, Marines are forward-thinking in their attempts to cement future roles for their Corps. The biggest challenge they face in doing so is figuring out the threat they will be facing. Former Commandant of the Marine Corps General C. C. Krulak described future force planning in the deceptively simple manner of a Marine. He said the three basic questions involved are: "Why will we fight, where will we fight, and whom will we fight?"

In the late 1990s, Marine intelligence officials were convinced that future combat would involve low-intensity regional conflicts, with terrorism as the primary tactic. It's important to remember that 9/11 hadn't yet happened, and the U.S.-led war on terrorism had not begun.

The Marine Corps has an intriguing future ahead indeed. Operation Iraqi Freedom, the ensuing occupation, and battles with insurgents demonstrated the need for leadership at all levels. The Marines have always stressed the importance of situational leaders, and they continue to set the standard.

More and more wars are being fought with asymmetrical warfare, which is placing an even greater emphasis on leadership. Asymmetrical warfare is nontraditional warfare using tactics such as improvised explosive devices and propaganda.

One of the most effective methods to combat these types of strategies is to disperse forces over a wide area, all the way down to the fire-team level. The fog of battle rarely existed so closely to diplomacy as it did in Iraq in the early twenty-first century. Even Marine PFCs are learning the fine balance between all-out fighting and shaking hands with the civilians.

Professor Leonard Wong, a twenty-year army veteran, discusses new trends among young army officers in his paper, "Developing Adaptive Leaders." The paper has relevance for the Marines as well. In it, he points out the emergence of leadership as a theme in civilian literature. For example, Warren Bennis, a leadership researcher, describes what he calls the crucible experience. Bennis' thought is that effective

leaders generally experience one powerful event that helps define exactly who they are. How they respond to such an event is a function of what Bennis calls "adaptive capacity," or how fast they produce smart responses to a state of change.

The Marines have always demonstrated a high degree of adaptive capacity. Even before the term was created in the pages of research findings, the Marines embodied the concept in everything they did. It's likely not much of a coincidence

المفوضية العليا المستقلة للانتخابات في العراق

كۆمیسیۆنی بالای سه‌ربه‌خۆی هه‌ڵبژاردنه کان له عێراق

The Independent Electoral Commission of Iraq

An Iraqi Security Forces soldier smiles while guarding the polling center during Operation River Gate. More than two thousand people voted on the constitution, which could decide the future of Iraq. Operation River Gate was the effort to conduct counterinsurgency operations with Iraqi Security Forces to isolate and neutralize insurgents, support the continued development of Iraqi Security Forces, and support Iraqi reconstruction and democratic elections to create a secure environment that would enable national self-reliance and self-governance.

that Bennis labeled the moment when character is defined as the "crucible experience." Each and every enlisted Marine goes through a fifty-four-hour crucible experience at the end of boot camp. Many of them will tell you that it was during that ordeal that they finally realized their full potential. As synonymous as the term "rifleman" is with the title "Marine," the expression "leader" is just as accurate. Marines don't just encourage each rifleman to seize opportunities; they expect it.

Existing skills of Marines are being broadened by the fact that they must usually pull double duty. They take on additional roles, and they do it with typical Marine Corps enthusiasm. All the while, they're absorbing Middle Eastern culture that helps them establish strong relationships when they need them.

The adaptability of the Marines will continue to be tested. As Professor Wong points out, the insurgents themselves are extremely adaptable. Plus, the modern battlefield can produce reliable intelligence quickly, which means that new missions arise sometimes very quickly.

Distributed operations, a concept born from the doctrine of maneuver warfare, are meant to capitalize on the experiences of the Marines on the front lines. Technology is being tested that will link entire battalions across the battlefield. As of January 2006, the system has seen limited use within the army. The thinking is that individual Marines can

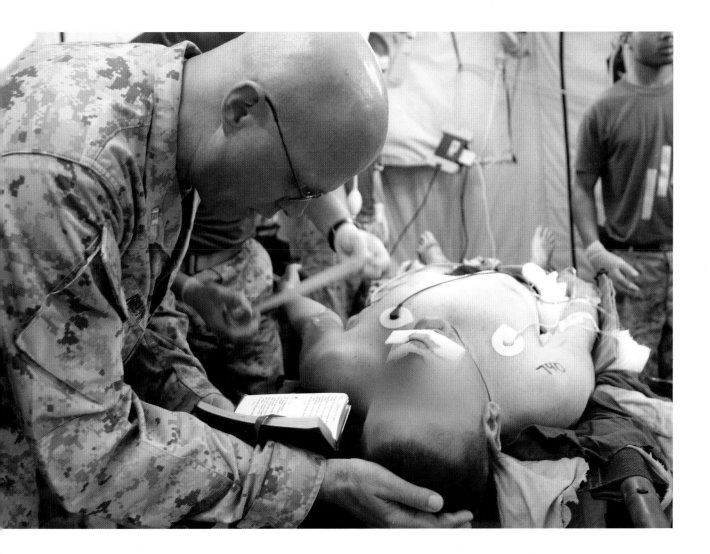

Medical personnel work with a severely wounded Marine as Chaplain Captain Nielson reads him his last rites.

Marines from Company G, 2nd Battalion, 2nd Marine Regiment, fire on terrorists in a truck who had launched rockets at them and then sped away. Riflemen, machine gunners, snipers, and mortarmen all gave the terrorists a taste of their own medicine during the hour of dusk.

be much more effective if they are aware of the entire situation that's unfolding around them.

The fluidity of events within combat takes on greater importance. As battle plans are altered, networked Marines will be able to use real-time situational analysis as a replacement for planning. One program under development in Arlington, Virginia, will help them make informed intuitive decisions. It's called the Command Post of the Future (CPOF), and Major Ryan Paterson, USMC, is one of its principal developers. CPOF is being designed with the vision of eliminating the need for a physical command post and making it a virtual reality instead. Everyone involved can follow any given situation, as well as help make decisions regarding planning and execution.

This experimental technology has tremendous implications for the Marines in future battles. They'll be able to record every move and every decision, as well as the results. Even in training, with the system in use, every method will be

stored away so that if a similar situation arises in live combat, the system will be prepared to offer suggestions.

Another concept in the works is sea basing. The plan is to give Marines the ability to carry out every stage of planning and buildup while still at sea. Once fully implemented, it will allow the Corps to put a Marine expeditionary brigade with a total force of about fifteen thousand Marines anywhere on the globe within twelve days. As an added bonus, sea basing results in fewer Marines on the ground, which helps the Marines honor the sovereignty of host nations.

New developments in the way the Corps fights battles will have significant implications behind the scenes as well. The Combat Service Support Element must innovate along with the gun slingers in order to adequately supply those on the front lines. In addition, with more and more humani-

Private First Class James Cardenas, an infantryman with 3rd Platoon, Company A, 1st Battalion, 5th Marine Regiment, provides security over a berm in Fallujah. The Marines assaulted the city to rid it of terrorists holed up inside.

Lance Corporal Brad McKee, an infantryman with 2nd Platoon, Company B, 1st Battalion, 6th Marine Regiment, directs traffic while patrolling the streets of Fallujah. The unit successfully confiscated numerous weapons and explosives, detaining several known insurgent supporters and helping Fallujah's residents rebuild their infrastructure.

tarian aid being delivered by Marines, it falls to the support crews to maintain the supply rates necessary for refugees and other noncombatants.

The Marine Corps is constantly striving to be a lighter, more agile force requiring less of a footprint within host nations, yet still able to fight well-armed enemies. The more mobile a force becomes, the more vehicles it usually requires. This, too, poses a problem, as moving large quantities of fuel over a great distance isn't easy, particularly if you then have to figure out how to disperse it over several spread-out destinations. Past and recent experiments have explored the possibility of alternative power sources; long-range rations, which would keep Marines fed for longer than the standard fifteen-day duration; and fuel-monitoring systems.

So, the challenge for combat service support units will be to find ways to keep up with the technology being implemented elsewhere within the Corps. They'll be continually asked to move more equipment and supplies faster and efficiently. They will also have to look at the sustainability of forces in a far broader scope than before. No longer will they be expected to support only quick-strike, over-the-horizon engagements. They must also develop the expertise to support long-term operations ashore.

The future of Marine aviation holds exciting possibilities as well. Among the highest priorities of senior aviation officials is the MV-22 Osprey program. Much maligned in its earlier stages of development due to some highly publicized accidents, the program is thriving. The intent is to replace the aging fleet of CH-46 medium transport helicopters with the MV-22s.

Very few similarities exist between the MV-22 and traditional helicopters; its transport capabilities and its ability to take off and land vertically are about the only ones. Other than that, the Osprey has the ability to leave helicopters behind in terms of both speed and range, so much so that even with planned improvements to the AH-1W Cobra and UH-1N Huey, much work lies ahead in order for these helicopters to provide the assault support to the ground troops delivered by the MV-22.

As of 2006, there are plans in the works to replace the uniquely Marine AV-8B Harrier and the F/A-18C/D Hornet with the short-takeoff, vertical-landing (STOVL) version of Joint Strike Fighter (JSF). While similar to other JSFs, the STOVL version will also provide the option of deployment from any number of navy ships, as well as many sites ashore. The JSF is scheduled to be in the fleet by 2010.

The Marine Corps has always done a lot with a little. As of 2005, they received only 6.5 percent of the total Department of Defense budget, but they were able to provide about 20 percent of the U.S. forces' combat power. Strategic spending has always been one of the hallmarks of the Corps' success. So, if they believe in the importance of cultural training for those about to be deployed, you know there's a good reason.

Senior officers within the Corps believe that this training will help young Marines gain an understanding of the enemies they're fighting, as well as the people they're helping. In-depth knowledge of enemies and their culture, they say, speeds the process of quickly finding and engaging them.

In earlier discussions of the MEU (SOC) within this book, it was stated that the Marines don't train separate

Lance Corporal Jacob Scott M. Barlass, a machine gunner with 4th Platoon, Company I, 3rd Battalion, 5th Marine Regiment, provides security behind the M240G machine gun on the streets of Al Kharma, Iraq.

Marines with 2nd Platoon, Company A, 1st Battalion, 5th Marine Regiment, search a car during a mission. The Marines captured an insurgent while conducting random vehicle and personnel searches throughout Ar Ramadi in an effort to capture insurgents and seize weapons. The man they caught was believed by Marine officials to be responsible for attacking Marines with improvised explosives.

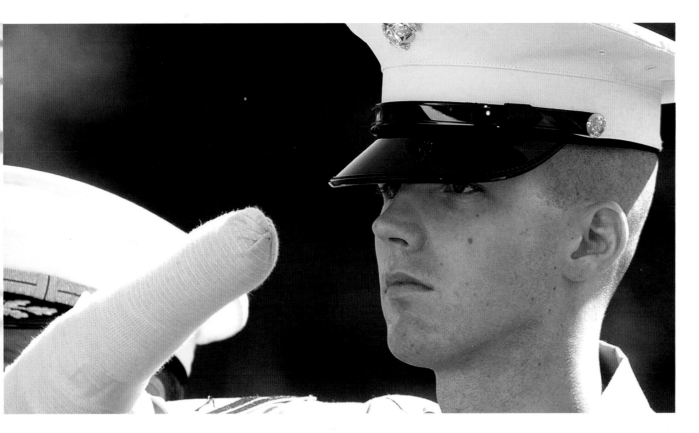

Opposite page: Lance Corporal Richard D. Poulis (left), machine gunner with 2nd Squad, 4th Platoon, Company B, 1st Battalion, 5th Marines, aims his weapon out of the window of an abandoned building and provides security for his fellow Marines while they conduct a weapons-cache search in an area on the outskirts of the city. Gunnery Sergeant Walter G. Siquieros was Poulis' senior drill instructor at Marine Corps Recruit Training Depot in San Diego. Siquieros became his platoon sergeant, and the two Marines supported Operation Iraqi Freedom together.

Above: Sergeant James Wright, who received the Bronze Star Medal with valor device from Deputy Defense Secretary Paul Wolfowitz, salutes during the national anthem at the June 1, 2004, presentation ceremony in front of the Marine Corps War Memorial in Arlington, Virginia. Wright lost both hands and suffered a severe wound to his leg when his vehicle was struck by an enemy rocket-propelled grenade in Iraq's Al Anbar Province. Despite his wounds, Wright continued to lead the Marines in his charge.

A Marine with 3rd Battalion, 4th Marine Regiment, pays his final respects to one of four fallen Marines. The battalion held a final memorial service honoring those who lost their lives during their deployment to Iraq.

special forces troops. However, there was some discussion early in the twenty-first century centered on the possibility of increasing their role within the special forces community. The war on terrorism expedited the talk, as more and more threats are being met by special operations. The math is simple: as more commitments involving special operations arise, the assets to carry out those commitments decline rapidly over time. In an attempt to begin such an integration of forces, some Force Recon Marines were reassigned to a special unit named Marine Corps Special Operations Command (MCSOCOM) Detachment One. But the questions that continue to be asked are about whether the Marines can make a unique contribution to special forces without degrading the expeditionary nature of their mission.

But most of all, the Corps' future looks strong due to the caliber of the young men and women they recruit. Even in the face of a difficult recruiting environment, the Marines have no intention of lowering their standards. So, as other branches continue to adopt more expeditionary practices, the Marine Corps will stay the course and keep doing things just like they have for the last 230 years.

Staff Sergeant Christian Harding watches a dark passageway while Lance Corporals Ambakisye Olutosin Smith and Paul Bauer watch another entrance of the World War II–era bunker during a clearing operation at Camp Lemonier, Djibouti, on October 14, 2005. Also known as Hills 74 and 43, these bunkers are located on the border of Djibouti and Somalia and are seen as possible terrorist insurgency threats. They are checked on a routine basis. *Air Force Staff Sergeant Stacy L. Pearsall*

Famous Battles in Marine Corps History

Battle of Chapultepec, September 12–13, 1847

Many Marines believe that without this famous battle, there may not even be a Marine Corps today. The men who fought and died during this battle are honored with two long-standing traditions. First, the blood stripe on the dress blue trouser worn by officers and noncommissioned officers commemorates those who died in taking the Mexican stronghold. It is a fitting tribute, considering 90 percent of the officers and NCOs who fought at Chapultepec also died there. And second, the opening words of the Marine hymn, "From the Halls of Montezuma," commemorate the Marine Corps' post-battle role of standing guard outside the Mexican Presidential Palace.

Battle of Belleau Wood, June 1–26, 1918

In one of the bloodiest battles in Marine Corps history, the American Expeditionary Force (AEF) was called in to launch a counterattack designed to stop the German advance. Their objective was to take the woods. To do so, they first had to cross an open field that left them all dangerously, in many cases mortally, exposed to one wave after another of German machine gun and artillery fire.

On their way across the field toward the woods, Americans crossed paths with thousands of French soldiers who were retreating. The French insisted that the Marines do the same thing. Captain Lloyd Williams' response would become an instantaneous addition to the USMC legend. He said, "Retreat, hell. We just got here."

While the objective of the fight was to take the woods, American forces actually had to do it six times before they were successful in driving the Germans out completely. When the bullets would run out, the Marines found new ways to fight. Many times it involved nothing more than their bayonets or fist-fights in hand-to-hand combat. But through it all, the Marines held their ground, and on June 26, 1918, a brief report was sent out that said it all: "Woods now U.S. Marine Corps entirely."

When it was all said and done, American forces suffered a total of 9,777 casualties, with 1,811 of them fatal. However, not only were the woods captured, but the German offensive was also brought to an end. The French honored all the U.S. forces by renaming the woods "Bois de la Brigade de Marine" ("Wood of the Marine Brigade"), and they awarded the 4th Brigade the Croix de Guerre. Even the Germans paid homage to them in reports afterward. One German called the Marines "vigorous, self-confident, and remarkable marksmen." General Pershing, commander of the AEF, said, "The Battle of Belleau Wood was for the U.S. the biggest battle since Appomattox and the most considerable engagement American troops had ever had with a foreign enemy."

Battle of Guadalcanal, August 7, 1942, to February 9, 1943

One of the most significant battles of World War II, the assault on Japanese-occupied Guadalcanal marked the first offensive by U.S. ground forces in the Pacific campaign. The Japanese had begun occupying the Solomon Islands one by one in an effort to cut off Allied shipping routes. Guadalcanal's position at the center of the chain of islands made it an easy choice to be the primary base. The Allies knew of Japan's plans and decided that defending their shipping routes would serve a valuable second purpose. By capturing Guadalcanal, they would have the perfect spot from which to assault Rabaul, north of the chain, where Japan already had a base.

Surprisingly, the Marines carried out an amphibious landing on the island on August 7, 1942, with little resistance from the Japanese. They secured an airstrip, and no one on the island even paid attention. But the Imperial Japanese Army did, and they sent reinforcements to take back the airstrip. The Marines met a battalion-size force at the Tenaru River. The Japanese attacked across the river's sandbars, and practically every one of the enemy soldiers was killed.

With the advantage of an airstrip, Marine aviators were able to protect the island and inflict heavy damage on the Japanese navy. So much so that control of that air field was the basis for much of the land combat that would soon follow.

By the middle of September, the Japanese army had regrouped and dispatched six thousand troops to attack the Marines in the middle of the night. The goal was to take back the air field, but after three days of fighting, the Japanese were forced to retreat. Once again, in October, the Japanese mounted an attack. This time they encountered fresh troops from the U.S. Army's 164th Infantry Regiment and the 1st Battalion, 7th Marines. This attack ended just like the first.

Then in November, the Japanese presented a strong show of force when they sent their 38th Infantry Division to take back the island. Along the way, however, they were met with heavy resistance during the Naval Battle of Guadalcanal. The division that went in came out of that battle numbering no more than a regiment. American forces continued to pound away at the Japanese to push the perimeter far enough back that the air field would no longer be within artillery range.

Over the course of the next couple of months, Japanese strength began to fade faster and faster thanks to the loss of soldiers and loss of supplies for those who remained. On February 8, 1943, the Japanese that remained on the island were evacuated, and the next day, American authorities declared Guadalcanal to be secure after six months of fighting.

Victory at Guadalcanal would be only the first of many invasions that led to the eventual assault on other Japanese islands. When the island was captured, it sent the clear message that the perimeter that Japan had established was not nearly as strong as they might have thought. The battle of Midway is often considered the turning point in the Pacific Theater. It's important to remember, though, that Japan's defeat at Midway was only naval in scope, so Guadalcanal is the battle that's credited with being the turning point for the Imperial Japanese Army.

Battle of Tarawa, November 20–23, 1943

Yet another one of the Marine Corps' defining battles that took place during World War II, Tarawa marked the second time the United States was on the offensive in that war. Unlike the first time, at Guadalcanal, the Marines faced serious opposition from the Japanese during their landing at Tarawa.

The United States knew that it would be impossible for its forces to support operations across the mid-Pacific, the Philippines, and into Japan itself without first taking the Marianas Islands. However, the Marianas posed a significant challenge, as they were very heavily defended and would need to be bombarded from the air before any troops could be sent in on the ground. The problem then became how to establish an intermediate base capable of launching the necessary air assets over the Marianas to carry out bombing. Due to various complications, it was decided that the best place to launch such an invasion of the Marianas would be well out to the east at Tarawa in the Gilbert Islands.

The Japanese had planned ahead for just such an invasion at Tarawa by fortifying the island with heavy artillery and twenty-six hundred of their most elite forces, the Imperial Marines. Japanese preparations included a system of trenches that allowed the troops to access any point on the island with some degree of cover. Additionally, they had cut an air field into the thick overgrowth higher up on the island. Concrete bunkers were well stocked around the island; some even contained eight-inch coastal defense guns brought in from Singapore.

Final preparations listed five hundred pillboxes, stockades of sorts, and forty pieces of heavy artillery at various positions around the island. In one of history's greatest examples of false bravado, Rear Admiral Shibasaki Keiji, garrison commander, bragged that it would take one million men one hundred years to conquer Tarawa. He must not have included the U.S. Marine Corps in his estimate, because it only took four days.

Knowing that the fight ahead would be tough, the American invasion force consisted of more assets than any other single operation before it. A total of seventeen aircraft carriers, twelve battleships, eight heavy cruisers, four light cruisers, sixty-six destroyers, and thirty-six transports represented more square footage than the objective they were headed for. Onboard were the 2nd Marine Division and a portion of the 27th Infantry Division, which gave the Americans a strength of thirty-five thousand soldiers and Marines. The 2nd Marine Division was to strike Betio in Tarawa Atoll, and the 27th Infantry Division was to hit Butaritari in Makin Atoll.

The battle began in the early morning hours of November 20, 1943. The naval gunships offshore hit the landing beaches with everything they had for over an hour and a half. The only lull in the action was to allow time for dive bombers to pound away at the larger guns, most of which had been destroyed during the barrage. So much of the narrow island was damaged by the initial assault that the Americans thought that there would be very little force remaining to defend what was left. But they had failed to consider the depths to which the Japanese had dug themselves into the island's hillsides.

Shortly after the Marines launched their attack, they found themselves stuck on a reef still five hundred yards from shore. They were open targets for the Japanese forces that were only then emerging from their dug-in bunkers. Before long, the boats caught on the reef were in flames due to Japanese fire. The troops inside jumped out to attempt the long trip ashore under constant machine gun fire. Any amtrac that was able to lumber over the reef was turned inside out by the large guns on shore. In fact, by the end of the day, more than half of them were out of action. Only a few men from the first wave were able to make it ashore, and they were trapped against the breakwater on the beach.

It would take many attempts to land tanks and break through the first line of Japanese defenses. But by noon on November 20, that's exactly what they had done. By 3:30 p.m., the line had progressed only slightly inland in just a few places.

However, once tanks landed successfully on the island, the line began to make progress, and by nightfall was almost halfway across the island.

As the next day dawned, the Marines were holding a strong line on the island and began using it as leverage to divide the Japanese forces. As that battle raged, the forces to the west of the island were given orders to secure the entire beach on that side of the island. Japanese soldiers were everywhere within the area, so the commander called in naval fire from offshore rather than fight them in direct combat. The strategy worked, as spotters slowly crawled forward to give coordinates for machine gun posts and other bunkers one at a time. Remaining defenses fell to the Marines within an hour and a half after the firing stopped.

Elsewhere on the island, the fighting was not going as smoothly, as it became evident that the Japanese had set up additional machine gun posts overnight. U.S. forces were able to bring in their own machine guns within a couple of hours, and soon the Japanese guns were out of commission. Nevertheless, by the end of the second day of fighting, the state of affairs was much as it had been at the end of the first day.

The western end of the island was under U.S. control, as was a good portion of the air field, with an almost continuous line of troops surrounding it. However, the groups were unable to contact one another, and there were large gaps between them. Yet, it was at that point that the Marines had captured the momentum.

On the third day of the battle, November 22, the primary objective of American forces was to consolidate their lines and bring more heavy equipment and tanks ashore. That afternoon, the 1st Battalion of the 6th Marines launched an offensive that soon found them chasing Japanese troops over the southern coast of the island. It didn't take long to join up with the forces that had landed on the eastern end of the air field two days earlier and to form a very important line of defense.

That night, the Japanese realized that there were very few places left for them to run. They consolidated their own forces and planned for a late-night counterattack. The small units that were sent in to soften U.S. positions were turned away, and the counteroffensive never happened.

Early on November 23, the assault that didn't happen the night before was finally staged. However, it was put to an end within an hour. The small pockets of forces that remained emerged during the night to continue fighting, but the island was securely in the hands of the Americans.

By battle's end, only 17 Japanese and 129 Korean laborers were alive. An estimated 4,690 Japanese troops and Japanese and Korean laborers were killed, while the U.S. forces lost 1,000 with an additional 2,200 wounded. Folks back home in America were outraged that so much devastation could take place over such a tiny, unimportant island. Yet the Marines know they don't always fight popular fights. They understand the importance of this battle to their own legacy, and they hold it up as one of their finest.

Battle of Iwo Jima, February 16 to March 26, 1945

A direct translation of the name Iwo Jima is "Sulfur Island." So why is a big hunk of sulfur so valuable, and how did it come to be the site of the most famous photograph in the world, particularly when you consider that the entire island is no more than eight square miles?

Early in 1945, the Allies were running bombing raids from the Marianas Islands to hit the mainland. Japanese soldiers basically turned Iwo Jima into an early-warning station. So by the time the bombers reached the mainland, the Japanese air defenses were waiting for them.

Thus, it should be no surprise that the Allies chose to invade the island rather than allow a two-month-long break in the action between the Battle of Leyte Gulf and an invasion of Okinawa. The landing at Iwo Jima was dubbed Operation Detachment.

As the Japanese were building their defenses on the island, they had accumulated over eighty fighter aircraft. But months before the actual battle would begin, the U.S. Navy played a significant part in assuring the victory. Surprising the Japanese, the navy bombed them for two days straight. Each and every building on the island was leveled, and the entire force of planes was reduced to just four. Without the possibility of air support, there was little chance that the Japanese would be able to defend themselves from a force with superior naval and air assets.

The planning for Operation Detachment was extensive. The primary objective was to increase the American hold on the Western Pacific by subjecting the Japanese to an almost constant barrage of military forces. Little did anyone know then that the landing on Iwo Jima would come to be known as "the classical amphibious assault of recorded history."

On February 19, 1945, at 2:00 a.m. D-day began with the thunderous roar of battleship guns. Shortly thereafter, one hundred bombers began their assault of the island, and as they cleared out, the naval guns took over where the bombers had left off. Then, at 8:30 a.m., the initial wave of what would eventually be thirty thousand Marines hit the shoreline. As they made their way onto the beach, the battle for Iwo Jima began.

The Japanese were dug deeply into Mount Suribachi. They unleashed one round of deadly fire after another as the Marines fought their way to the summit a few feet at a time. Using rifles, ayonets, their fists, and the occasional flamethrower, it took the Marines four days to reach the summit. And it was at that moment that Associated Press photographer Joe Rosenthal captured one of the most famous images in American history.

"Raising the Flag on Iwo Jima" depicts the American flag being planted on the mountaintop. Rosenthal said that he didn't think he had gotten the picture because he just picked up his camera and clicked the shutter. He wasn't even looking through the eyepiece. Many Americans think the image represents the victorious ending to the battle for Iwo Jima, but it actually raged for another month. A couple of the men who raised the flag didn't even make it off the island. Those who did found their lives forever altered due to their association with the picture.

The Marines were sent in to capture the island to use it as an American air base. They ended up doing so before the battle even ended. The B-29 bomber dubbed *Dinah Might* by its crew was dangerously low on fuel near the island and requested an emergency landing. Under heavy fire from enemies who took exception to an American plane using their airstrip, the bomber nonetheless landed on the area of the island under American control. Routine maintenance was performed, fuel was taken on, and the plane flew away, without incident.

The fighting was so intense that over the course of the thirty-eight-day battle, the original thirty thousand Marines ashore had to be supplemented by forty thousand more. Many Medals of Honor were awarded to Marines in World War II, and over a quarter of them were earned on Iwo Jima: twenty-seven in total. As for the Japanese, they began the battle with twenty-two thousand entrenched soldiers. By the end of the fighting, only two hundred or so had survived to become enemy prisoners of war. The Americans suffered twenty-six thousand casualties of their own, including seven thousand dead. So it should be no wonder Admiral Chester E. Nimitz summed up their effort by saying, "Among the men who fought on Iwo Jima, uncommon valor was a common virtue."

Battle of Chosin Reservoir, November 26 to December 13, 1950

By all accounts, the Korean War was just about over. North Korea was almost completely held by UN forces with Americans at the helm. Then, in mid-October 1950, the Chinese joined the fight when they crossed the Yalu River and surrounded the UN troops at the Chosin Reservoir.

The unexpected battle pitted roughly 20,000 UN forces against 200,000 very well organized but very poorly prepared Chinese soldiers. With numbers like that, the Americans had no choice but to order a retreat, which became a fighting withdrawal to the south, toward Hungnam. Along the way, 2,500 died, 5,000 were wounded, and 192 were listed as missing. An additional 7,500 suffered cold-related injuries.

Even with superior weapons and air assets, the UN forces were devastated by the sheer number of Chinese soldiers. But on their way to Hungnam, the Americans dealt their share of blows. The Marines proved that a "fighting retreat" was not the same thing as a retreat. Of the 200,000 Chinese, 25,000 were killed and 12,500 more were wounded.

In addition to the 1st Marine Division, the 7th Infantry Division of the U.S. Army was also present for the fight. However, when the 7th Division retreated, they abandoned their equipment. The 1st Marines, British Royal Marines, and the South Korean Marines recovered the army's equipment and used it during an all-out assault to force their way out of the reservoir.

Lieutenant General O. P. Smith, the commanding officer of the 1st Marine Division, adamantly believed that his Marines were not retreating. When pressed to explain his reasoning, General Smith's answer was abbreviated to the famous misquote, "Retreat, hell! We're attacking in a different direction."

Even though they were withdrawing, the Marines had the advantage of air power on their side. They used it to decimate all seven divisions of the Chinese army that were pinning them in the reservoir. Still, they were able to hold together long enough to force the fighting retreat.

Over the course of the two and a half weeks at Chosin Reservoir, the Marines found help in some unexpected places. For example, Chinese-American Marines were able to translate Chinese battle plans that they overheard on the battlefield. So while they were fighting in retreat and losing many Marines along the way, they were able to inflict more casualties than they suffered on their way out. Despite the losses they suffered, Marines for years to come will point to this battle as a proud chapter in their history. Even with the odds stacked so heavily against them, the Marines simply don't have it in them to walk away from a fight, much less to retreat.

Each and every Marine carries the success and the loss of these and every other battle in their hearts. It becomes a part of their very fabric, and it's the strongest fiber of their collective morale. "Once a Marine, always a Marine" is more than a slogan or a bumper sticker. Recruit training and officer candidates school change young men and women. They become a part of something bigger than themselves. They discover a crystal-clear purpose. They are prepared to defend it at all costs. And we, as a nation, are lucky to have them on our side. Semper Fi, Marines, you all do great work.

Battle for Baghdad, Episode 5, Shootout!, 2005, TV, History Channel, August 23, 2005.

Battle of Belleau Wood, Wikipedia.org, The Free Encyclopedia; modified October 29, 2005; text available under GNU free documentation license.

Battle of Chosin Reservoir, Wikipedia.org, The Free Encyclopedia; modified November 7, 2005; text available under GNU free documentation license.

Battle of Guadalcanal; Wikipedia.org, The Free Encyclopedia; modified November 5, 2005; text available under GNU free documentation license.

Battle of Iwo Jima, Wikipedia.org, The Free Encyclopedia; modified November 8, 2005; text available under GNU free documentation license.

Battle of Tarawa, Wikipedia.org, The Free Encyclopedia; modified November 9, 2005; text available under GNU free documentation license.

Clancy, Tom, 1996. *Marine: A Guided Tour of a Marine Expeditionary Unit*, New York, NY, Berkley Books.

D-Day: Fallujah, Episode 1, Shootout!, 2005, TV, History Channel, July 19, 2005.

Fisher, Cindy, 2005. CMC: "Changes in Corps' Future Will Benefit Marines' End-Strength, Restructure to Increase Crucial Capabilities: Big Changes Are on the Horizon for the Marine Corps." *Marines Magazine* [online edition].

Halberstadt, Hans, 1993. *U.S. Marine Corps*, Osceola, WI, MBI Publishing Company.

Howe, Neil & Strauss, William, 2000. *Millenials Rising: The Next Great Generation*. New York, NY, Vintage Books.

Iraq's Ambush Alley, Episode 9, Shootout!, 2005, TV, History Channel, November 1, 2005.

Jarrell, Kit, April 12, 2005. Re: First Sergeant Brad Kasal *euphoricreality.net* [online]. Available from http://www.blackfive.net/main [accessed November 10, 2005].

Krulak, Former Commandant C. C., USMC, 1997. *Warfighting* Quantico, VA, United States government.

Owens, Mackubin T., 2005. *Iwo Jima and the Future of the Marine Corps*. Editorial. Ashbrook Center for Public Affairs at Ashland University.

Paterson, Major Ryan, USMC, 2005. Capturing Live Combat in Network Centric Warfare. *DarpaTech 2005*, August 9-11, 2005.

Ricks, Thomas E., 1997. *Making the Corps*, New York, NY, Simon & Schuster.

Storm, Sergeant Robert M., 2005. *Marines Repel Ambush in Afghanistan* [online]. Korengal Valley, Afghanistan, MCB Hawaii. Available from www.usmc.mil [accessed November 11, 2005].

Swanson, David & Galloway, Joseph L., 2004. Battle at Ramadi, *The Philadelphia Inquirer*, August 15, online edition. Available from www.philly.com [accessed November 8, 2005].

Swofford, Anthony, 2003. *Jarhead: A Marine's Chronicle of the Gulf War and Other Battles*. New York, NY, Scribner.

Wong, Leonard, 2004. *Developing Adaptive Leaders: The Crucible Experience of Operation Iraqi Freedom*. Monograph. Strategic Studies Institute (SSI).

Unknown, 2003. *Marine Corps Mortuary Affairs* [online] Marine Corps News Service. Available from http://usmilitary.about.com/cs/marines/a/mortuary.htm [accessed November 14, 2005].

Index

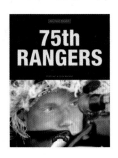
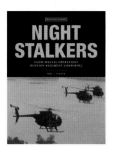

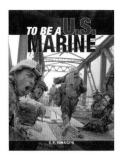

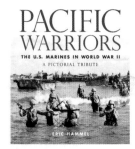